Test Your English Usage I.Q.

WORD WISE:

I hope I did not (**imply/infer**) by my actions that I hated your idea about adding guacamole-raisin crunch to our roster of ice cream flavors.

PRONOUN PARANOIA:

The woman (**that/who**) came to dinner last night was my sister Eileen.

VICIOUS VERBS:

If this (**was/were**) a well-run camel caravan, we wouldn't be lost.

POINTS WELL TAKEN:

Last night's dinner consisted of goose liver, leg of lamb (**comma, no comma**) and dessert.

Find the Right Answers in Your Own User-Friendly Guide:
GRAMMAR FOR SMART PEOPLE™

■

"Some people read dictionaries and grammar books for fun. But some people like anchovies on their pizza, so there's no accounting for taste. Author Barry Tarshis tries to make *GRAMMAR FOR SMART PEOPLE* more like pepperoni pizza. He largely succeeds. . . . He is not hidebound about the rules of grammar. . . . He tries for useful and usable guidelines that writers not only can use but will *remember*. He also tries to inject humor whenever possible."

—*Indianapolis Star*

"*GRAMMAR FOR SMART PEOPLE* is useful whether you're taking English this year or going back to your twentieth-anniversary reunion, where your grammar teacher will trap you by the cheese dip and administer a pop quiz."

—*Memphis Commerical Appeal*

GRAMMAR
FOR SMART
PEOPLE™

Your User-Friendly
Guide to
Speaking and Writing
Better English

BARRY TARSHIS

Illustrations by R. J. Matson

POCKET BOOKS

New York   London   Toronto   Sydney

POCKET BOOKS, a division of Simon & Schuster Inc.
1230 Avenue of the Americas, New York, NY 10020

Tarshis, Barry.
    Grammar for smart people : your user-friendly guide to speaking and
writing better English / Barry Tarshis.
        p.   cm.
    ISBN: 0-671-75044-5
    1. English language—Grammar—1950–   I. Title.
PE1112.T37   1992
428.2—dc20   92-17453
                                                                          CIP

First Pocket Books trade paperback printing September 1993

20 19 18 17 16 15 14 13

POCKET and colophon are registered trademarks of Simon & Schuster Inc.

Printed in the U.S.A.

Acknowledgments

The number of friends, colleagues, and family members without whose help, judgment, and encouragement this book would never have been written is in the dozens, but I would like to extend a special thank-you to the following people: to Richard Seclow, whose early support was the catalyst that led to the original Grammar for Smart People self-study program (and the company I founded); to the 12 other people (Les Becker, Fred Berg, Robert Bogart, Jan Dauman, David Diamond, Denny Davidoff, Sheldon Fireman, Richard Gold, Mike Goodman, Chuck Halper, Charles Lobel, and Leslie Raffel) who became partners in Grammar for Smart People Inc.; to John Boswell, my agent, who encouraged me to write the book and helped me develop the original proposal; to his associate Patty Brown, whose vigilant editing of the early drafts made the book much better than it would have otherwise been; to Julie Rubenstein and Molly Allen, of Pocket Books, for their thoughtful and intelligent support (and for being such a joy to work with); to R. J. Matson, for his brilliant illustrations; to my associate and good friend, Roy Speed; and, finally, to all the members of my family (Karen, Lauren, Andrew, David, and Leo), who, throughout this project, have shown more support, love, and patience than I could have ever hoped for.

Contents

GRAMMAR
FOR SMART
PEOPLE ™

Introduction

There is a tendency among people who teach or write about grammar to treat the subject as though it were a green vegetable: You may not like grammar, in other words, but it's good for you. And the reason it's good for you, if you will excuse my celebration of the obvious, is that the image you project (translation: how smart people think you are) depends in large part on how smoothly you handle the English language.

But enough lecturing. I learned very quickly when I first began conducting writing seminars more than ten years ago that you don't have to do much sermonizing about the importance of using proper grammar to people whose livelihoods depend in large part on how well they communicate. And I don't think it's necessary to do much preaching in the introduction of this book. The fact that you have either bought or are thinking about buying this book suggests that you do not need to be sold on the idea of becoming more comfortable with the basics of English. What you need to know is whether *Grammar for Smart People* offers you something you can't get from the scores of other grammar and usage books now on the market.

I think it does.

Grammar for Smart People has evolved out of a series of courses and seminars that my company, Grammar for Smart People Inc., runs for corporations and other organizations seeking to do something about the way their employees or students speak and write English. As with any course on grammar or writing, our objective is to teach people how to speak and write English more effectively. What makes us different, however, is our approach. We don't think it is good business to make adults feel as if they're back in sixth grade, and so we go out of our way to make sure that the topics we cover are relevant to adults, and, in particular, to adults in the workplace; and we go out of our way, too, to present the basic principles of grammar in a manner that is lively, challenging, and—dare I say it?—*fun.*

My goal in this book is no less ambitious. What I have tried to do—and what I think I've done—in *Grammar for Smart People* is to write a guide to speaking and writing better English that does more than simply rehash the same litany of "rules" and "principles" that have been talked about, written about, argued about, and sweated over for centuries. I have tried to organize the book in a manner geared to the way people actually *use* the language, and I have done my utmost to make this book not only accurate but easy to access, easy to understand, and easy—and enjoyable—to read. What I have tried to do, in short, is to produce a true *user's* guide to speaking and writing better English in the 1990s.

Having said all this, let me point out quickly that neither this book nor any of the programs and courses my company has developed are meant to be the definitive word on grammar and usage. English grammar is a monolithic and sprawling subject, and if you were so inclined, you could devote the better part of your lifetime to studying a tiny segment of it—the gerund, let's say. On the reasonably safe assumption that most people are *not* so inclined, I have focused my attention in this book on those specific grammar and usage issues that are the most relevant to everyday speech and writing—and, more important, on those issues that are the most frequent sources of uncertainty, confusion, and debate.

I have also put more emphasis in this book on *what* you should do if you want to speak and write English more effectively and less on *why* it is grammatically incumbent upon you to do so. Yes, many of the usage guidelines in this book are supported by explanations that involve a grammar principle. But whenever I have felt the need to clarify a usage guideline with a grammar principle, I have done my best to keep the explanation brief and to the point. I have also done my best to keep the number of grammar terms in this book to a manageable minimum, resisting, however, the trend among some grammar instructors today to avoid traditional grammar terminology entirely. (The idea of teaching people grammar without using the traditional grammar terms— nouns, verbs, adjectives, etc.—*sounds* intriguing, but I've tried it and I don't think it works: It's like teaching surgery without obliging students to learn the names of the organs the students will be removing or repairing.)

In any event, whenever I have used a grammar term in any listing, I have put it in SMALL CAPITALS—an indication that a definition of the term appears in the Glossary portion of the Appendix. I have also included in the Appendix a short section that covers eight of the bedrock principles of English grammar. If you have forgotten these principles (quick test: Can you name the seven main parts of speech?) or went to a school in which, for whatever reason, these principles were purposely *not* taught to you, I would urge you to look over the Appendix before you plunge headfirst into the book itself.

One other aspect of *Grammar for Smart People* warrants discussion. I'm talking here about the rationale I have used for the usage guidelines that appear throughout the book.

It is worth mentioning that if this were a book about French or Italian grammar, it wouldn't be necessary to discuss or defend the rationale behind these usage guidelines. That's because usage standards in French and Italian are regulated by powerful and highly respected language academies that have been in existence for nearly four centuries and that count among their members the elite of each country's language scholars.

For better or worse, and despite repeated attempts since the seventeenth century to establish one, there is no English counterpart to these academies—no single group, book, or individual specifically empowered to police the way the language is spoken and written. This is not to suggest that there are no usage standards in English or that nobody cares about the state of the language. There *are* standards, and people *do* care. The problem, though, is that the people who care don't necessarily agree with one another about which standards ought to prevail, and there is no organized mechanism in English for resolving these differences. Consequently, once you get beyond the basics (or what *Webster's Dictionary of English Usage* describes as "opinions . . . that have been with us long enough to be regarded as rules"), the question of whether a particular way of expressing an idea is good or bad English is ultimately a matter of taste and judgment, or, to be more specific, the taste and judgment of a specific writer, teacher, editor, lexicographer, or grammarian who has had the gumption or the arrogance to proffer an opinion.

I, too, like everyone who writes about language, have my own views of how English ought to be spoken and written, but I have resisted the temptation to impose these views on my readers. What I have tried to do instead is to make each guideline in the book represent the *collective* view of the dozen or so usage authorities listed in the Bibliography. In so doing, I have tried to strike a fair balance between those authorities who favor a strict interpretation of traditional grammar principles and those who would give the language a longer leash, allowing acceptability to be determined by the way the language is actually used, as opposed to the way grammarians think it *ought* to be used.

For the record, my own position in this ongoing debate is somewhere in the middle of these two extremes. I am willing to accept as a fixed part of English usage most of the grammar basics that were drilled into me when I attended grade school in the 1950s, but I am not one of those ultra-constructionists who would advocate corporal punishment for people who dare to split infinitives or end sentences with prepositions. By the same token, I share the belief that usage standards should be flexible enough to reflect our changing lifestyles, but I don't think we should update our dictionaries as frequently as we update phone directories, and I'm not one of those anti-traditionalists who would banish usage standards altogether on the grounds that such standards are, at root, a form of elitism or snobbery.

The most sensible approach to this entire issue, I

think—and the one I have taken in this book—is to view the way we speak and write English as a form of social behavior, much like our eating or grooming habits. We all have the right to eat with our hands, slurp our soup, and traipse around in clothing that hasn't been laundered in weeks. But if we exercise that right in public, we have no right to feel insulted or persecuted when people view us as ill-mannered or uncouth.

Similarly, we all have the right to express our ideas however we see fit, without having to worry about stepping on the toes of grammarians who set their views on paper more than four hundred years ago. But given the fact that most people *accept* a particular usage principle as the norm, when we flout that principle in public—and particularly in a business setting—it would be naive to think that people will not take notice and will not judge us in ways we may not want to be judged.

If *Grammar for Smart People* does nothing else, it will give you a better understanding of the usage standards most literate people subscribe to in the 1990s, and it will give you the knowledge and the understanding you need to incorporate those standards into your own usage decisions. For this reason alone, I think you will find *Grammar for Smart People* a valuable book. I would hope, too, that using this book will not only enhance your appreciation of English but will also give you more confidence in your ability to *use* the language more effectively in your business and your personal life.

CHAPTER 1

Word Wise

How to put the proper word in its proper place

This chapter deals with verbal abuse. More precisely, it deals with those words and expressions in English that in the view of most usage authorities are common sources of confusion and misuse.

As it happens, the number of words and expressions in English that fall into this dubious category is substantial. But that is to be expected, given the nature of the language. Forget for the moment that English has more words per se than any other of the major languages of the world, or that it is more densely populated than other languages with words that have foreign origins. Focus instead on the fact that English, as William Safire has pointed out, is a "stretch language"—a language, in other words, that gives its users an enormous amount of elbow room when the time comes to express ideas. No other language, on the one hand, has as many words that mean the same or nearly the same thing, and, on the other hand, has as many words that take on different meanings in different situations.

All this elbow room, of course, is terrific news if you are one of those persons who loves words and would just as soon go to bed with a good dictionary as with a Robert Ludlum thriller; but it is not terrific news if you are concerned about using what Jonathan Swift liked to call "the proper word in its proper place." For how do you know, given all the choices you have in any given situation, which word is, in fact, the "proper" word: the long word, the short word, the more formal word, the idiomatic word, the word Shakespeare used, the word your boss uses, ad infinitum?

The purpose of this chapter is to help you answer that question when you are dealing with those words and expressions (and most of them, not surprisingly, come in pairs) that, for a variety of reasons, have become troublesome to most people. In many of the listings that follow, the choice is clear-cut: Similar though the words may look or sound, they mean different things. More often than not, however, the words in each listing are close enough in meaning that a case could be made for either choice; and in a few instances the only difference between the two words or expressions is that one of the choices grew up in a bad neighborhood and hasn't yet achieved enough respectability to be considered standard English.

With these considerations in mind, I have based the guideline in each listing on how the majority of today's better writers, editors, and usage authorities would handle the choice in each pairing, and I have relied, in particular, on two sources: *The American Heritage Dictionary* and *Webster's Dictionary of English Usage*. I have also divided the word pairings into several categories, based not only on *why* the words are confused, but on how significantly they differ in their basic meanings. (Note: All the words listed appear alphabetically in the Index.)

The listings themselves consist of a usage guideline and a sentence or two that illustrate the distinction at the heart of the guideline. Some of the listings include a sentence or two that further clarify the distinction; and where I thought it might help, I have included a memory key—an easy-to-remember sentence or phrase designed to help you keep in mind the distinction between the two words.

A final word about the mechanics of this chapter— and, for that matter, the book itself. You will notice as you read through this chapter that in some cases parenthetical information is enclosed within brackets [ ] while in other cases it is enclosed within parentheses ( ). I have used brackets primarily for definitions inserted in the examples to help reinforce the distinction between the two words. I have used parentheses for everything else.

Sore Thumbs

A random sampling of those words and sets of words that deserve special attention, given how frequently they are misused

ADVERSE & AVERSE: Up against it

Guideline. Use *adverse* (never followed by *to*) to describe reactions that are unfavorable, hostile, and unfortunate. Use *averse* (generally followed by *to*) to suggest the idea of being *against* something.

> Even though I had an <u>adverse</u> [unfavorable] reaction the first time I tasted the guacamole-raisin-crunch ice cream, I have changed my mind and am no longer <u>averse</u> to [against] the idea of introducing the flavor next summer.

Memory key. Never ADd to an ADVERSE reaction.

AFFECT & EFFECT: Influence game

Guideline. Use *affect* (almost always a VERB) when expressing the action that means "to influence" or "have an impact upon." Don't confuse it with either the NOUN form of *effect*, which means "result," or with the verb form of *effect*, which means to "produce a result."

> The speech Dimitri gave after dinner last night had a strong <u>effect</u> [impact] on all of us, especially Inga.

> Inga's tearful reply to Dimitri's speech <u>affected</u> [had an influence on] us even more.

And:

> Thanks to the conversation we had with Dimitri, we were

able to *effect* [bring about] a major change in the plan in a matter of hours.

A closer look. *Affect* can operate as a noun, but only as a psychological term. It is used to differentiate a feeling or an emotion from a thought or action.

Memory key. To keep in mind that *effect* is usually a noun, remember the phrase NOW IN [noun] EFFECT.

AMONG & BETWEEN: Beyond the numbers

Guideline. Use *between* when you are drawing a connection involving only *two* persons or things. Use *among* when *three* or more persons or things are involved.

> Jesse and Frank were hoping to divide the money *between* the two of them [only two involved], but Billy and Cole wanted the money to be distributed *among* all the people [more than two involved] who took part in the project.

A closer look. *Between* is appropriate to use when you are drawing a connection involving three or more persons or things that are interacting with or being compared with one another on a one-to-one basis.

> When you put aside their age differences, there is really no difference *between* Jesse, Frank, Billy, and Cole. (The suggestion is that Jesse, Frank, Billy, and Cole are being compared with one another: Jesse with Frank, Jesse with Billy, Billy with Cole, etc.)

AS & LIKE: Wrong connection

Guideline. Don't lose sleep over which of these two words is proper to use in conversation. In writing, however, favor *as* when it is being used as a CONJUNCTION and is followed by a CLAUSE (a group of words that includes a subject and its verb). Use *like* when it is operating as a PREPOSITION.

> The fish that Nero served last night was excellent, <u>as</u> it always is when Octavius does the cooking. (The group of words following <u>as</u> is a clause, whose subject is <u>it</u> and whose verb is <u>is</u>.)

> It looks <u>as if</u> Brutus will support the plan. (The group of words following <u>as if</u> is a clause, whose subject is <u>Brutus</u> and whose verb is <u>will support</u>.)

But:

> The fish that Nero served last night looked a lot <u>like</u> speckled trout. (<u>Like</u> is a preposition. Its object is <u>trout</u>.)

> The plan we have devised looks <u>like</u> money in the bank. (<u>Like</u> is a preposition. Its object is <u>money</u>.)

BAD & BADLY: Feeling things out

Guideline. Use *bad* when it modifies a NOUN or when it follows a LINKING VERB, especially *feel* or *look*. Use *badly* when it operates as an ADVERB.

> I feel <u>bad</u> about what happened last night after all the king's horses left. (<u>Feel</u> is used here as a linking verb; it joins with <u>bad</u> to show a state of being, not an action.)

I didn't think the king's men did too _badly_, considering the shape the egg was in. (_Badly_ operates as an adverb, modifying the verb _did_.)

Things don't look nearly as _bad_ as they did when I first heard about the egg falling off the wall. (_Look_ is used here as a linking verb, which calls for an adjective.)

A closer look. In conversation you can usually get away with saying "I feel _badly_ . . . ," but not when you're breaking bread with grammar purists. For more on the difference between linking and action verbs, see page 165.

Memory key. We FEEL BAD when we perform BADLY.

CAN & MAY: Permission granted

Guideline. Use _can_ when you mean the _ability_ to do something. Use _may_ when you are seeking _permission_ or using the word as a synonym for _might_.

May [permission] I borrow your crystal ball?

Can [ability] you reach it from where you are sitting?

I think I _can_ [am able], but there's a chance I _may_ [might] spill my coffee if I try to get it.

A closer look. There is no difference grammatically between "How _may_ [might] I help you?" and "How _can_ I [am I able to] help you?" _May_ sounds more polite, but either is standard English.

Memory key. If you get MAY's PERMISSION, leave the CAN on the tABLE.

GOOD & WELL: The right feeling

Guideline. Use *good* when the sentence calls for an ADJECTIVE (especially after the LINKING VERB *feel*). Use *well* when the sentence calls for an ADVERB, but with one key exception: when you are describing the state of someone's health.

> The king's men worked *well* together. (*Well* is an adverb modifying the verb *worked*.)

> Everyone feels *good* about the plans we have made for next week's camel caravan. (*Good* is an adjective that follows the linking verb *feel*.)

> But:

> Unfortunately, I missed last night's tuba concert. I wasn't feeling too *well*. (The sentence is talking about health.)

Memory key. If you feel GOOD about your work, you will usually do WELL.

HOPEFULLY: An open question

Guideline. Think twice before using *hopefully* at the beginning of a sentence as a shorter way of saying "Let us hope." Hold your criticism of people who don't share your restraint.

> *Let us hope* that [not *hopefully*,] the weather will hold for tomorrow's tango contest.

> But:

> We are looking forward *hopefully* [in a hopeful manner] to a successful tango contest.

A closer look. The case against using *hopefully* as a shorter version of "Let us hope" is based on the argument that as an ADVERB it needs a VERB to modify. But only a handful of usage authorities continue to argue the case, and *hopefully* as a sentence opener seems to have worked its way into legitimacy.

IMPLY & INFER: Giving and receiving

Guideline. Use *imply* when you mean "suggesting" something or "giving an impression." Use *infer* when your meaning is to "assume," "interpret," or "draw a conclusion."

> I hope I did not *imply* [suggest] by my actions at the meeting yesterday that I hated your idea about adding guacamole-raisin-crunch to our ice cream flavors.

> As I watched you wincing and gnashing your teeth, I naturally *inferred* [assumed] that you were not thrilled with my idea.

Memory key. The carpenter SUGGESTS PLYwood.

ITS & IT'S: Bad marks

Guideline. Use *it's* as a CONTRACTION for *it is* (and be careful where you stick the APOSTROPHE). Use *its*—without an apostrophe—as the POSSESSIVE form of *it*.

> *It's* [It is] too early to tell how the plot will turn out and what *its* [possessive] impact will be on Dimitri's future in the company.

A closer look. Unlike NOUNS, which rely on the APOSTROPHE to show possession, PRONOUNS have their own possessive forms. There are no apostrophes in the possessive pronouns *my, his, hers, ours, yours,* or *theirs.* You don't need one for *its.*

Memory key. ITS SITS alone as an owner.

LAY & LIE: Resting places

Guideline. Use *lie* to express the act of reclining, resting, or simply sitting somewhere. Use *lay* to express the act of setting something down. Be careful about how you express the PAST TENSE of each word.

> Jesse, I would like you to *lay* [set] that pistol down, mosey into the bedroom, and *lie* [recline] down on the bed.

> At the same time that George was *laying* [setting] down the law about keeping confidential material in the vault, Dimitri's file was *lying* [sitting] on the desk.

A closer look. The grief created by these two words (reportedly the two most frequently misused words in English) is rooted in what happens to each of them in their PAST TENSE and PAST PARTICIPLE forms. *Lay* becomes *laid* (not *layed*) in the past tense, and *have, had,* or *will have laid* in the PERFECT TENSES. *Lie* in the past tense becomes—get ready!—*lay,* and in the perfect tenses becomes *have, had,* or *will have lain.*

> After Jesse *laid* [past tense of *lay*] his pistol down, he moseyed into the bedroom, and *lay* [past tense of *lie*] down on the bed.

> The last I heard, Jesse *had laid* [past perfect form of *lay*] his pistol down, had moseyed into the bedroom, and *had lain* [past perfect form of *lie*] down on the bed.

PRINCIPAL & PRINCIPLE: Making headway

Guideline. Use *principle* when referring to things you can believe in or follow—rules or standards of behavior. Use *principal* when referring to either people (the *principal* of a school or the *principals* in a company) or money (the *principal* on a loan). As an ADJECTIVE, use *principal* to indicate prominence and importance.

> The *principal* [head of our high school] talks often about the *principles* [rules] that have guided him throughout his career. That's the *principal* [main] reason I do not enjoy spending time with him.

Memory key. My PAL, the PRINCIPAL, believes in simPLE PRINCIPLES.

THAN & THEN: A matter of when

Guideline. Use *than* to connect the two parts of a comparison. Use *then* to denote a point in time.

> Inga was more ambitious four years ago *than* [comparison] she is today. Back *then* [when], however, she wasn't as interested in Dimitri.

Memory key. THAN like AND connects. THEN shows WHEN.

THEIR & THERE & THEY'RE: Sound-alikes

Guideline. Use *their* as the POSSESSIVE form of *they*, *there* as an ADVERB that means the opposite of *here*, and *they're* as a CONTRACTION of *they are*.

> Based on the conversations I have had with Cassius and Casca, *there* is every reason to believe that *they're* going

to give us *their* full cooperation. We won't know for certain, however, until we are actually *there* in Rome.

A closer look. In the commonly used "There is . . ." construction, *there* operates as something known as an EXPLETIVE—a word whose main role is to smooth out the syntax of a sentence.

WHO, THAT, & WHICH: Relatively speaking

Guideline. Use *who* when referring to people. Base your choice between *that* and *which* on whether the RELATIVE CLAUSE that either word introduces is RESTRICTIVE *(that)* or NONRESTRICTIVE *(which)*. (For more on these three words and more on restrictive and nonrestrictive clauses, see page 162.)

> We are looking for someone *who* can tell us about what happened last night at the wall after the king's horses went home. (*Who* refers back to a person—*someone*.)

> The egg *that* fell off the wall last night could not be put back together. (The clause introduced by *that* is restrictive. It is needed to identify which specific egg the sentence is talking about.)

> Last night's incident, *which* I have spoken to you about, was the third such incident in a week. (The clause introduced by *which* is nonrestrictive. It is not needed to identify the incident being referred to.)

Worlds Apart

Frequently confused words that mean entirely different things

ALL READY & ALREADY: Well prepared

Guideline. Use *already* as an ADVERB to show that something has happened previously. Use *all ready* to give emphasis to "being set."

> We were *all ready* [all set] to give up hope when we learned that Dimitri had *already* [it has happened] arrived in Bratislava.

Memory key. AL was READY ALREADY when I arrived.

ALLUDE & ELUDE: A slippery distinction

Guideline. Use *allude* when your meaning is to "draw attention to something indirectly or in passing." (See also *Allude & Refer*, page 31.) Use *elude* when your meaning is to "escape," "avoid," or "evade."

> Owen *alluded* [made vague references] several times to the jobs he did when he was working for Nero, but made no mention of how he was able to *elude* [evade] Nero's bodyguards and escape to Naples.

A closer look. The NOUN to use when referring to what you have *alluded* to is *allusion*. The ADJECTIVE used to describe somebody (or something) who *eludes* is *elusive*, which means the same thing as "slippery." There is no such word as *elusion*.

ANECDOTE & ANTIDOTE: One man's poison

Guideline. Use *antidote* to describe the medicine you would take if you were bitten by a poisonous snake—or to describe anything you might do to counteract the effects of something threatening or unpleasant. Use *anecdote* to describe the short (and, one would hope, interesting) story about what happened to you.

> Whenever he comes to dinner, Uncle Ned likes to spin a lot of _anecdotes_ [stories] about his boyhood in Alaska.

> I find that one of the best _antidotes_ [medicines] to the dinners I have with Uncle Ned is to drink a lot of wine.

APPRAISE & APPRISE: Keeping up

Guideline. Use *appraise* when your meaning is to "determine the value or extent of." Use *apprise* when you're looking for a fancier way to say "tell."

> As soon as the insurance adjustor _appraises_ [evaluates] the damage the egg suffered when it fell off the wall, I will _apprise_ [tell] you of your options.

Memory key. VALUE the PRAISE of an APPRAISER, but don't be surPRISED when you are APPRISED of the fine print.

ARBITRATE & MEDIATE: A question of authority

Guideline. Use *arbitrate* to describe the work of someone who listens to evidence from both sides of a dispute and then makes a binding decision. Use *mediate* to describe the efforts of someone who is there to play peacemaker but has no authority to impose a settlement.

The mellow monkey called in to _mediate_ [try to make peace] the territorial dispute between the lions and hyenas has failed to make peace. Now an arbitrary aardvark has been brought in to _arbitrate_ [make a binding decision] and to settle the issue once and for all.

Memory key. A MEDIATOR MEETS. An ARBITRATOR twists ARms.

AWHILE & A WHILE: Mean whiles

Guideline. Use _awhile_ when you want an ADVERB that means "for a short time." Use _a while_ when the expression is preceded by _for._

I listened _awhile_ [for a short time] to Marc Antony's speech, but I got nervous when the crowd began to turn on Brutus.

After the speech, Dimitri and I stayed for _a while_ with Inga and talked about Marc Antony's speech.

CAPITAL & CAPITOL: This old building

Guideline. Use _capitol_ in two situations only: one, when you are referring to the _Capitol_ building in Washington (in which case the word is a PROPER NOUN and should always be—well, _capitalized_); two, whenever you mention any of the buildings in which state legislatures conduct their business. In all other situations, use _capital._

Harrisburg, the _capital_ [seat of government] of Pennsylvania, is seeking _capital_ [money] to fund a bridge that will run from Ohio to New York. The decision will be reached tomorrow in the _capitol_ [building].

Memory key. The CAPITOL is an OLd building.

CLIMATIC & CLIMACTIC: Final act

Guideline. Use *climatic* (without the *c* in the middle) when referring to the weather. Use *climactic* when referring to the climax of an event.

> The *climactic* [culminating] point of the day came when the king himself came to look at the egg. Unfortunately, *climatic* [weather] conditions forced him to leave sooner than expected.

Memory key. The CLIMACTIC moment in a play usually comes in the final ACT.

COMPLEMENT & COMPLIMENT: Finishing touches

Guideline. Use *complement* when referring to something that adds the finishing touches to something else. Use *compliment* in connection with praise or flattery, and use *complimentary* as a SYNONYM for "at no cost."

> I would like to *compliment* [praise] you on the tango contest you held last night at the end of the party, and I want to thank you for the *complimentary* [free] tickets to next year's contest. The tickets were an ideal *complement* [finishing touch] to a wonderful evening.

Memory key. Associate the E in COMPLEMENT with COMPLETE.

COVERT & OVERT: Night and day

Guideline. Use *covert* when the behavior you're describing is secret. Use *overt* to describe behavior that is open and obvious.

Opposition to Dimitri's plan to open an ice cream parlor in Bratislava has been _overt_ [open]. Everybody knows about it.

There has been a _covert_ [secret] effort to close down the work we are all doing on the Lunar Tides and Productivity Project. I have no idea who is behind this effort.

Memory key. Associate COVERT with COVER, and OVERT with OVERTURE.

CREDIBLE & CREDITABLE: A matter of confidence

Guideline. Use _credible_ when you want to describe somebody or something as believable. Use _creditable_ to describe something or somebody you consider worthy of praise.

The witness gave a _credible_ [believable] account of what happened after the king's horses arrived, and the police did a _creditable_ [praiseworthy] job of keeping the crowd calm after the king's horses had gone.

Memory key. CREDITABLE people deserve CREDIT.

DISCREET & DISCRETE: Quiet separation

Guideline. Use _discreet_ when you mean "prudent" and "showing good judgment." Use _discrete_ when your meaning is to keep things "separate."

Inga and Dimitri have always been _discreet_ [prudent] about their relationship. Even so, we need to keep our concern about their relationship _discrete_ [separate] from the concerns we have about the plan.

A closer look. Don't be confused by the fact that the NOUN counterpart to *discreet—discretion—*has only one *e.*

Memory key. DISCREET people kEEp secrets.

DISINTERESTED & UNINTERESTED: Getting involved

Guideline. Use *disinterested* when you mean "objective" and "impartial." Use *uninterested* when you mean "indifferent" or "bored."

> I don't mean to be cynical, Your Honor, but I find it hard to believe that you can remain *disinterested* [impartial] when the prosecuting attorney is your daughter-in-law.

> I spent a few minutes watching the trial; however, after Socrates's speech I became *uninterested* [bored] and turned off the set.

EMIGRATE & IMMIGRATE: Coming and going

Guideline: Use *immigrate* to convey the idea of coming to a new country and setting down roots. Use *emigrate* to describe what you do when you decide to leave a country with the idea of never going back. You *immigrate to* and *emigrate from.*

> Dimitri's mother and father *immigrated* to [came to] the United States in 1981 from Moscow. Two years later they *emigrated* from the U.S. and went to Afghanistan, where they felt more comfortable with the climate, the language, and the ice cream flavors.

ENERVATE & ENERGIZE: Energy crisis

Guideline. Use *enervate* to describe a person or experience that has left you exhausted. Use *energize* to describe a person or experience that has left you full of energy.

> Working closely with Hamlet has been fun but *enervating* [tiring]. I've never been so exhausted in my life.

> The meetings with Brutus and Cassius have been both fun and *energizing* [exciting]. I've never had more energy in my life. Cinna, in particular, is a stitch.

FAMOUS & INFAMOUS: A matter of reputation

Guideline. Use *famous* to describe anybody who has achieved wide renown. Use *infamous* to describe *famous* people with notorious reputations.

> Dimitri is *famous* [well known] for his ability to create interesting ice cream flavors, but is *infamous* [notoriously bad] for his clumsiness on the dance floor.

Memory key. INFAMOUS is an INsulting term.

FIGURATIVELY & LITERALLY: In a manner of speaking

Guideline. Be careful about using *literally* when you are making a *figurative* or symbolic point. *Literally* means "actually" and "within the strict meaning of"; it should be used sparingly when you want to emphasize a point.

> I was astonished to discover that there are people in our company who *literally* [actually] do not know the names of the ice cream flavors we manufacture. (Correctly used

because the fact is that a lot of people in the company do not know the names of the company's ice cream flavors.)

But not:

When I heard that so many people in our company do not know the names of the ice cream flavors we manufacture, I *literally* blew up. (Less precisely used because if you had *literally* blown up, you wouldn't be around to describe your reaction.)

FLAMMABLE, INFLAMMABLE, & NONFLAMMABLE: Grounds for firing

Guideline. Never use *inflammable* to describe something that is fireproof. *Inflammable* means the same thing as *flammable*. Things that *can't* catch fire are *nonflammable*.

I am not surprised the tent burned as quickly as it did: The material was highly *inflammable* [combustible]. The next tent I buy will be *nonflammable* [fireproof].

FLAUNT & FLOUT: Showing off

Guideline. Use *flaunt* to describe the actions of people who like to show off. Use *flout* to describe the actions of people who openly defy authority or rules.

Octavius visited us last week so that he could *flaunt* [show off] his new chariot. He proceeded to *flout* [ignore] the local regulations by parking it directly in front of the Gucci outlet, near the Coliseum.

Memory key. If you FLOUT, you operate OUTside the law. If you FLAUNT, you waNT to show off.

FORMER & LATE: Deadly mistake

Guideline. Use *former* to refer to somebody, still alive, who used to fill a particular role or do a particular job. Use *late* to refer to people who have died recently, regardless of what they did when they were living.

> Gladys Peck, our *former* [at one time] plumber, was elected to the state legislature last week. (*Former* indicates that Gladys is still alive but no longer our plumber—at least until the next election.)

> Gladys Peck, our *late* [recently deceased] plumber, always wanted to be a politician.

Memory key. If we're LATE for the meeting, we're DEAD.

INCREDIBLE & INCREDULOUS: Lie detectors

Guideline. Use *incredible* to describe anything that defies belief, but keep in mind that in conversation the word is usually used to describe something that actually happened and was fairly sensational to boot. Use *incredulous* to express skepticism or doubt.

> The jury members found the defendant's description of the events that took place in Rome that morning too *incredible* [impossible to believe] to take seriously.

> Now that I have had a chance to review all the facts, I am more *incredulous* [skeptical] than ever about Plautus's ability to keep Nero under control, violin lessons or no.

But:

> That was certainly an *incredible* [remarkable] group of people at Petrarch's house the other night.

INGENIOUS & INGENUOUS: Idiot savants

Guideline. Use *ingenious* to describe someone who is bright, resourceful, imaginative, and filled with inventive ideas. Use *ingenuous* to describe someone who is guileless and naive.

> It is hard to imagine that someone as innocent and as *ingenuous* [naive] as Inga could have invented such an intricate and *ingenious* [clever] plot.

Memory key. A GENIus comes up with INGENIOUS ideas.

MARITAL & MARTIAL: Shotgun weddings

Guideline. *Marital* relates to marriage. *Martial* relates to military matters. Don't use them interchangeably unless you're doing it intentionally.

> One of the ways Marisa has been able to put up with the *marital* [marriage] problems she has been having with Mario over the past two years is to have become a master in the *martial* [military] arts.

Memory key. Associate RITe with MARITAL, and ART with MARTIAL arts.

PROSTATE & PROSTRATE: Prone to lie

Guideline. Use *prostate* when you are referring to the male gland located in the urethra. Use *prostrate* to describe what you do when you kneel in front of someone or lie flat on the ground.

> When Dimitri learned that he didn't need an operation on

his *prostate* gland, he was so relieved that he *prostrated* himself in front of the doctor.

Memory key. Associate PROSTRATE with lying STRAight.

RESPECTFULLY & RESPECTIVELY: Keeping order

Guideline. Use *respectfully* when you want to describe an action that is respectful and deferential. Use *respectively* to coordinate the order in which a number of things have been mentioned.

Everyone acted *respectfully* [with respect] throughout the initiation ceremonies.

The lead and the supporting roles were played by Robert Redford and Al Pacino, *respectively*. (Redford played the lead, and Pacino played the supporting role.)

But not:

Romeo and Juliet were played by Al Pacino and Michelle Pfeiffer, *respectively*. (No need for *respectively* since the order doesn't need further clarification.)

SIMPLE & SIMPLISTIC: Too much of a good thing

Guideline. Use *simple* to describe something that's easy, uncomplicated, or unaffected. Use *simplistic* to describe something so simplified that it is no longer useful.

The instructions that came with the new left-handed javelin were clear and *simple* [easy to understand].

I found the advice we received in the course on how to

throw the left-handed javelin *simplistic* [oversimplified]: It was a lot harder to throw than the instructions suggested.

Memory key. Something too SIMPLISTIC is not REALISTIC.

Shades of Meaning

Pairs of words that are close enough in meaning to get confused but different enough to keep distinct

ABILITY & CAPACITY: Fixing limits

Guideline. Use *ability* when describing a power or skill you can develop. Use *capacity* to describe an existing state or potential.

A closer look. *Ability* is usually followed by an INFINITIVE. *Capacity* is usually followed by the PREPOSITION *for.*

Your *ability* [power] to become a world-class tuba player is often limited by your lung *capacity* [potential].

When he's not sitting there just brooding, Hamlet has a marvelous *capacity* for enjoyment and the *ability* to find humor in almost every situation.

Memory key. There's a CAP on CAPACITY but not on ABILITY.

AGGRAVATE & IRRITATE: Making things worse

Guideline. Favor *irritate* when the meaning you want to convey is to "annoy" or "provoke." Use *aggravate* when your meaning is to "make a bad situation worse."

Uncle Ned's lengthy stories at dinner last night *irritated* [provoked] all of us and *aggravated* [made worse] the tension that had been building ever since he arrived.

ALL TOGETHER & ALTOGETHER: Altogether different

Guideline. Use *altogether* when you mean "entirely" or "all told." Use *all together* when you mean "assembled" or "all in a group."

Altogether [all told] there were about twenty of the king's men and twenty horses, and they were *all together* [assembled] in one group when the trouble began.

Memory key. I am ALTOGETHER pleased that this ASSEMBLY brings us ALL TOGETHER at the same time.

ALLUDE & REFER: Reference points

Guideline. Use *allude* (see also *Allude & Elude*, page 19) when you are drawing attention to something in an oblique manner. Use *refer* when the mention is direct.

Inga *alluded* [hinted at] several times to her life in Bratislava, but *referred* [mentioned] only once to Dimitri.

ANTICIPATE & EXPECT: Waiting game

Guideline. Use *expect* when you are talking about something that is simply likely to occur. Use *anticipate* when you're looking forward to this likelihood with excitement and interest, or, better, when you have taken some action in preparation for what is about to happen.

We are *expecting* [view as likely to occur] about twenty people to attend this year's tango contest.

We are *anticipating* [looking forward with great excitement] the largest crowd we've ever had at our annual tango contest. (*Expect* could work here, too, but *anticipate* carries with it an idea that goes beyond simple expectation.)

We have *anticipated* [taken preparatory action] the arrival of a large crowd by hiring extra ushers.

ANXIOUS & EAGER: Pins and needles

Guideline. Stick with *eager* when you are looking forward to something but aren't worried about it. Use *anxious* when the situation is anxiety-provoking.

I am *eager* [looking forward] to get started on the Lunar Tides and Productivity Project, but I am *anxious* [a little worried] about certain aspects of the schedule.

A closer look. Using *anxious* to mean "earnestly desirous" has become common practice in spoken English and is grammatically defensible (if barely) in written English.

ASSURE, ENSURE, & INSURE: Making certain

Guideline. The meaning at the core of all three words is to "make certain," but each has its own wrinkle. *Assure* works best when its OBJECT is a person. *Insure* is best used when the idea in the sentence is "prevention." *Ensure* (usually followed by *that*) works in most other situations.

I am hoping that my proposal to add some interesting new ice cream flavors to the cafeteria menu will <u>assure</u> you that we mean business when we talk about improving employee morale. (The object of <u>assure</u> is <u>you</u>, a person.)

The plan I am recommending will <u>insure</u> us against the threat of employees quitting because they hate the food. (<u>Insure</u> is used here because the idea in this sentence is "prevention.")

These recommendations should <u>ensure</u> that our company maintains its reputation as having the best employee cafeteria in Bratislava. (<u>Ensure</u> is used here because the meaning is "make certain.")

Memory key. You INSURE by using an INSURANCE company. You ASSURE by giving ASSURANCES to people.

AVERT & AVOID: Evasive action

Guideline. You *avert* a situation by taking some action that prevents it from occurring. You *avoid* a situation simply by staying away from it.

The coolheadedness of my camel driver <u>averted</u> [prevented] what could have been a frightful situation.

Because of what happened during my camel ride, I intend to <u>avoid</u> [keep away from] the desert for a few months.

BRING & TAKE: Coming and going

Guideline. Use *bring* when the act of carrying or escorting is directed toward the speaker or to a place normally identified with the speaker. Use *take* when the act of carrying is moving away from the speaker.

> When you go to Rome, *take* this violin to Nero. (action away from the speaker)

> If he gives you a check, *bring* it back to me as soon as you can. (action toward the speaker)

Memory key. If you BRING ME a present, I'll TAKE you AWAY to someplace nice.

CENSOR & CENSURE: Faultfinders

Guideline. Use *censure* to describe the act of criticizing or assigning blame, especially when it occurs in a public setting. Use *censor* to describe the act of examining something—a book, a movie, a television show, etc.—with the idea of removing from it any elements considered objectionable, obscene, or secret.

> Several of the senators have been publicly *censured* [criticized] for the letter they wrote to Dimitri, but the contents of the letter have been *censored* [kept from public view].

COINCIDENCE & IRONY: A question of fate

Guideline. Use *coincidence* to describe the chance occurrence of two events at the same time. Use *irony* when the situation carries with it an element of contradiction or incongruity—of something happening that no one expected to happen.

> It was quite a *coincidence* [chance occurrence] for Dimitri and Inga to find themselves on the same train.

It was *ironic* [an incongruous turn of events] that Dimitri and Inga found themselves on the same train together the day after they had vowed never to see each other again.

A closer look. An *ironic* statement means something other than its literal meaning. A not especially subtle example would be saying "Nice weather, isn't it?" in the middle of a hurricane.

COMPARE TO & COMPARE WITH: Side by side

Guideline. Use *compare to* when your purpose is simply to liken—to point up the similarity (or dissimilarity) between—two things. Use *compare with* when your purpose is to analyze two things on the basis of their similarities or differences.

You cannot begin to *compare* [liken] tango dancers *to* flamenco dancers.

I would like to begin my speech by *comparing* [weighing one against the other] this year's tango dancers *with* the dancers we had last year.

COMPRISE, IS COMPRISED OF, & INCLUDE: Filling up

Guideline. Use *comprise* when you mean to "consist of" (as opposed to "are the elements of"). Use *include* when you are mentioning or listing some or most (rather than all) of the items in a series. Think twice before using *is comprised of* for anything.

The new training kit *comprises* [consists of] a videotape, two audiocassettes, and an autographed photograph of the emperor.

Or:

The new training kit _includes_ [has, in addition to other things,] an autographed photograph of the emperor.

But not:

The new training kit _is comprised of_ [should be _is composed of_] a videotape, two audiocassettes, and an autographed photograph of the emperor.

A closer look. _Is comprised of_ has become so commonly used as a synonym for "consists of" that many usage guides now consider the phrase standard.

CONTINUAL & CONTINUOUS: Stop and go

Guideline. Use _continuous_ when describing something that keeps going on, without stopping. Use _continual_ when describing something that goes on frequently, but in fits and starts.

The flamenco dancers who live upstairs from me have been rehearsing _continually_ [on and off] over the past three days.

The flamenco dancers who live upstairs rehearsed _continuously_ [without stopping] last night. I didn't sleep a wink.

CONVINCE & PERSUADE: Influence game

Guideline. Use _convince_ when your meaning is to "win people over to your point of view." Use _persuade_ when your argument gets them to change their minds or their actions.

Cassius has *convinced* all of us [made us believe] that Caesar is getting too big for his boots, but we have not yet been *persuaded* [motivated] to do anything about it.

I could probably be *persuaded* [swayed] to take part in next week's tango contest if you could *convince* me [make me believe] that I won't have to dance with Dimitri.

A closer look. *Convince* and *persuade* can usually be used interchangeably when the CLAUSE that follows is introduced by *that* or *of. Persuade* is the better choice when the clause that follows is introduced by *to.*

Memory key. A PERSUASIVE argument SWAYS people to act.

DEPRECATE & DEPRECIATE: Downsizing

Guideline. Use *deprecate* when your meaning is to "belittle" or "express disapproval." Use *depreciate* when your meaning is "to lessen the value of."

Nothing *depreciates* [lessens] the value of an apartment more than having a troupe of flamenco dancers living above you. Still, I am afraid to say anything to Manuel because he will think I am *deprecating* [criticizing] his life's work.

FARTHER & FURTHER: Going the distance

Guideline. Confine your use of *farther* to references involving physical distance. Use *further* in all other situations.

How much *farther* do we have to go before we reach the oasis?

I refuse to discuss this matter any *further* [more] until I hear from Dĩmitri and Inga.

FEWER & LESS: Diminishing returns

Guideline. Use *fewer* when referring to a number of items or persons. Use *less* when referring to a single amount.

There was *less* space [a single amount] on the dance floor than I thought, but there were also *fewer* dancers [a number of items].

FORTUNATE & FORTUITOUS: Fortune cookies

Guideline. Use *fortuitous* to describe those events that happen by chance. Avoid its use as an all-purpose SYN-ONYM for *fortunate*, which can be used to describe situations or events that are either planned or unplanned.

It was *fortunate* [a good thing] that we had enough time after last night's tango contest to iron out some of our differences. And how *fortuitous* [a lucky thing] it was that we bumped into Dimitri on our way home.

HISTORIC & HISTORICAL: Worth noting

Guideline. Use *historic* to describe any event that marks a milestone. Use *historical* when that event—or any event you may be referring to—warrants mention in a history book.

I understand that Brutus picked up the check after last night's *historical* society [people interested in history] meeting. What a *historic* [monumental] occasion.

IF & WHETHER: Chances are

Guideline. Use *if* when you're expressing a single condition. Use *whether* when the condition involves two possibilities. If you're using *whether*, you can usually omit the *or not*. Exception: when you want to give equal emphasis to both possibilities.

> *If* [only one possibility] it rains next Friday, the tango contest is off.

> *Whether* [two possibilities: rain or no rain] it rains next Friday is not my concern.

> *Whether* it rains next Friday or not, the plan is still on. (Equal emphasis is given here to the possibility of rain occurring or not occurring.)

IN BEHALF OF & ON BEHALF OF: Interested parties

Guideline. Use *in behalf of* when your actions are designed to benefit somebody. Use *on behalf of* when you are acting as somebody's representative.

> I know I am speaking *on behalf of* [as a representative for] everyone in our company when I tell you how pleased I am to be making this contribution *in behalf of* [in the interests of] the Retired Gladiators' Fund.

LEND & LOAN: Borrowed time

Guideline. Use *lend* as the VERB that means to "give on a temporary basis," and *loan* to describe whatever it is you are giving.

> Friends, Romans, Countrymen, *lend* me [not *loan* me] your ears.

LET & LEAVE: Alone together

Guideline. Use *leave* and *let* interchangeably as long as you follow each word with *alone*. Otherwise, use *leave* when your meaning is to "go away," or "not to take something with you," and use *let* when your meaning is "allow."

> I don't care how you handle the arrangements for the coronation, as long as you *let* [don't bother] me alone.

But:

> We decided to *let* [allow] Cassius talk to Brutus.

> I had no choice but to *leave* [not take it with you] the violin behind in Rome.

LIABLE & LIKELY: Looking ahead

Guideline. Use *likely* when you're dealing strictly with likelihood. Use *liable* when that likelihood involves a possibly unhappy outcome.

> The way things look now, we're *likely* to be [should be] finished with all the tango contest plans by next Friday. (likelihood and no danger)

> If you're not careful when you're sitting on the wall, you're *liable* [in danger of] to get hurt. (danger but not necessarily likelihood)

> If you're not careful when you are sitting on the wall, you are *likely* to hurt yourself. (both danger and likelihood in this situation)

NAUSEOUS & NAUSEATED: Gut reactions

Guideline. Use *nauseated* to describe a queasy feeling in your stomach. Use *nauseous* to describe the person or thing that made your stomach queasy in the first place.

> Not long after I started watching the tango contest, I suddenly felt *nauseated* [sick].

> The first three contestants put on a *nauseous* [sickening] display of tango dancing.

ORAL & VERBAL: Word of mouth

Guideline. Use *verbal* to refer to anything involving words, whether the words are written or spoken. Use *oral* to differentiate the spoken word from the written word.

> I had an *oral* [spoken] agreement with Dimitri, but we seem to have had some *verbal* [word] confusion over its content.

A closer look. Even though *verbal agreement* is generally understood to mean an agreement reached without a written contract, *oral* is the more precise term for this situation.

QUALITATIVE & QUANTITATIVE: Value judgment

Guideline. Use *quantitative* to describe investigative data that represent something measurable, like numbers. Use *qualitative* to describe data that deal with general characteristics.

> Surveys can yield valuable *quantitative* [hard] data, but you can also gain some good *qualitative* [softer] data by

interviewing the survey takers, who get roughed up by the people who are asked embarrassing questions.

RELUCTANT & RETICENT: Close to the vest

Guideline. Don't use *reticent*, which means "tight-lipped" and "reserved," as a synonym for *reluctant*, which means "hesitant" and "not favorably disposed."

> At first, I was *reluctant* [hesitant] to say anything that might have offended the emperor. Then again, I have always been *reticent* [quiet] whenever the emperor has asked me to offer my opinion about his violin playing.

VENAL & VENIAL: Shady dealings

Guideline. Use *venal* to describe anybody who is a ripe candidate for bribery. Use *venial* to describe minor sins—the kind that are easy to forgive.

> Lucius is not nearly as *venal* [corrupt] as he used to be before he was arrested for bribing Nero's barber. The sins he commits today are *venial* [minor] and hardly worth talking about.

Memory key. We should PENALize VENAL public officials.

Overkill

Expressions that include words you don't need

ALL OF: Except for us

Guideline. Except when the phrase is followed by a pronoun, you don't need the preposition *of*.

All the king's horses and _all_ the king's men couldn't figure out how to put the egg back together.

All of us at the ashram are quietly awaiting your return.

CONSENSUS OF OPINION: Too many cooks

Guideline. Don't use _of opinion_ when you're using _consensus_. The meaning of the word _consensus_ is "collective opinion."

The _consensus_ is that Inga and Dimitri will win this year's tango contest hands down.

FROM WHENCE: Where it stops

Guideline. Use _whence_ (if thou must) as a synonym for "from what place." You don't need _from_.

Even though they are very nice, I would love to see the flamenco dancers who live above me go back to _whence_ [from where] they came.

THE REASON IS BECAUSE: Why do it?

Guideline. Avoid the use of _because_ after _the reason is_. It's a redundancy, albeit one that is in common use.

The _reason_ we can't meet at Brutus's house tonight is _that_ [not _because_] he and Portia are having house guests.

A Question of Grammar

Words whose misuse revolves around a grammar principle

A & AN: Vile errors

Guideline. Use *a* before any word that begins with a CONSONANT sound. Use *an* before any word that begins with a VOWEL sound.

> I thought that Inga did *an* outstanding job of convincing Dimitri that we needed *a* better escape plan.

But:

> I doubt if the oasis is more than *an* hour's ride from here, but only if we follow *a* U-shaped route. (The *h* in *hour* is silent; *U-shaped* is pronounced "Yoo-shaped"—a consonant sound.)

And:

> What *a* [or *an*] historic occasion. (Whether you use *a* or *an* before *historic* depends on which side of the Atlantic you're on. In England, where the *h* in *historic* has a softer sound, the word is usually preceded by *an.* In the U.S., the *h* has a more vigorous sound, making *a* the more accepted choice.)

AS, BECAUSE, & SINCE: Ongoing problem

Guideline. Use *because* or *since* when you might otherwise say "the reason being." Use *as* when you would otherwise use "during."

> I didn't hear any of the commotion that went on last night *because* [the reason being] I was fast asleep.

I didn't get a chance to see any of the king's men <u>as</u> [during the time] they were marching by very quickly.

Different from:

I didn't get a chance to see any of the king's men <u>because</u> [the reason being] they were marching by very quickly.

DIFFERENT FROM & DIFFERENT THAN: Marked distinctions

Guideline. Favor *different from* in most cases, but keep in mind that *different than* is now considered acceptable in many situations.

Dimitri is <u>different from</u> the way I imagined he would be, based on his photograph.

But:

The situation is a lot <u>different</u> today <u>than</u> it was last night during the tango contest. (The alternative here would be wordier: "The situation is a lot different today from the way it was last night during the tango contest.")

DUE TO, BECAUSE OF, & OWING TO: Just cause

Guideline. Use these phrases interchangeably, but be prepared to defend your use of *due to* when it follows an ACTION VERB.

A closer look. *Due to* fell into disrespect in the early 1900s, when grammarians decided it was an ADJECTIVE and therefore could not modify an action verb. Some usage authorities still hold that position, but the modern view is that *due to* is a PREPOSITIONAL PHRASE and can therefore be used wherever you feel like using it.

> My foul mood this morning is _due to_ the argument I had last night with the flamenco dancers who live above me. (_Due to_ is standard here because it follows a linking verb, _is._)

> I didn't sleep a wink last night _due to_ [or _because of_, or _owing to_] the noise created by the flamenco dancers who live above me.

GRADUATED & WAS GRADUATED: School's out

Guideline. Don't worry any longer about the differences that might have once separated these two ways of saying the same thing. *Graduated* is the more widely used.

> Dimitri _graduated_ [or _was graduated_] from the University of Bratislava in 1965.

IRREGARDLESS & REGARDLESS: Double indemnity

Guideline. Pretend that *irregardless* doesn't exist.

> We will be holding the tango contest this year _regardless_ of what happens in Bratislava.

WOULD HAVE & WOULD OF: Mistaken identity

Guideline. Never use *would of*; it's always *would have*.

A closer look. This error crops up frequently because the contraction for *would have (would've)* sounds a lot like *would of.*

> We _would have_ loved to have heard last night's tuba concert.

Avoiding Pronoun Paranoia

How to <u>know</u> when you're right

-MATSON

Pronouns are those remarkably handy little words (*I, it, who, this,* etc.) that spare us the trouble of having to repeat the actual name of a person, place, or thing each time we refer to it. Handy as they are, however, pronouns are common stumbling blocks in English—even for the grammatically sure of foot. And given the nature of pronouns, it's no wonder.

The main problem with pronouns is that the ones we use the most frequently—personal pronouns—are inflected. That is, their forms change from one situation to the next. *I*, *me*, and *my* all refer to the same person, but you can't use these words interchangeably, as if they were mix-and-match dinner plates. Each form—like the forms that spring from *you*, *he*, *she*, *they*, and *who*—has its place. And to put the proper form of the pronoun in its proper place, you need to know something about the way sentences work, and you need to know something about the different roles that pronouns can play in a sentence.

It could be a lot worse. The complications that make pronouns tricky to handle in English are minuscule compared to the complications that bedevil the student of German, a language so densely inflected that the second-person pronoun alone—*you*—can be expressed in seven different ways. In English, you never have more than three pronoun forms to choose from in any situation. And the proper choice among the three is usually so obvious that most of us have pretty well figured out the script by the time we've learned to tie our shoes—long before we're aware of the grammatical implications of our choices. We learn it the old-fashioned way: by ear.

Which, unfortunately, is one of the problems with pronouns. For while you can usually tell, simply by the way a particular form of the pronoun *sounds*, if you're using it correctly, your ear can nonetheless lead you astray in certain situations.

These are the situations we will be focusing on in this chapter. First, though, a brief introduction to pronoun use in general.

The Basics of Proper Pronoun Usage

Using the proper form of a personal pronoun presupposes your ability to handle the following tasks—either consciously or automatically.

1. Identify the pronoun's ANTECEDENT.
2. Make sure the pronoun agrees with its antecedent in PERSON, GENDER, and NUMBER.
3. Recognize what CASE the pronoun is in.
4. Choose the right form of the pronoun based on its case.

If the message in the previous four sentences is familiar to you, you can go directly to page 52, which focuses on the pronoun situations that create special problems. Otherwise, it would be a good idea to spend a moment looking over the explanations that follow.

Pronouns at a Glance
Terms worth knowing when you're dealing with pronouns

The antecedent

The ANTECEDENT of a pronoun (sometimes referred to as the *referent*) is the word or words for which the pronoun substitutes. In the sentence "Every dog has his day," the antecedent of the pronoun *his* is *dog*. In the sentence "Cassius and I have completed *our* travel plans," the pronoun is *our* and the antecedents are *Cassius* and *I*.

A basic rule of pronoun usage is that pronouns must AGREE with their antecedents in person, number, and gender. Just as basic, however, is the need to construct your sentences so that there is no doubt about which word or words are the antecedents of the pronoun.

Person

PERSON is the term used to distinguish the person actually doing the speaking *(first person)*, from the person being spoken to *(second person)*, from the person (or thing) being spoken about *(third person)*. Pronouns and verbs are the only two parts of speech in which person has grammatical significance. The categories and their corresponding pronoun forms are as follows:

First person: *I, me, my, mine, we, us, our, ours*

Second person: *you, your, yours*

Third person: *he, him, his, she, her, hers, it, its, they, them, their, theirs*

Number and gender

NUMBER refers to whether the antecedent represents one person, place, or thing (singular) or more than one (plural). GENDER, of course, refers to sex: whether the antecedent is considered masculine, feminine, or neuter.

Case

CASE refers to what function the pronoun is performing in a sentence. These functions are usually divided into three categories, with each category having its own forms. The categories are as follows:

■ **Subjective case.** A pronoun is in the subjective case

(and thus uses the subjective case form) when it is the SUBJECT of a VERB or is linked to the subject by a LINKING VERB.

I could have been a contender. (*I* is in the subjective case because it is the subject of the verb *could have been*.)

They died with their boots on. (*They* is in the subjective case because it is the subject of the verb *died*.)

It is *I* who could have been a contender. (*I* is in the subjective case because it is linked to the subject [*It*] by a linking verb [*is*].)

■ **Objective case.** A pronoun is in the objective case when it is the OBJECT of a VERB or a PREPOSITION.

Several of the tango dancers asked *me* about Dimitri. (*Me* is in the objective case because it is the object [technically, the indirect object] of the verb *asked*.)

Inga doesn't like the way Dimitri behaves when he dances and doesn't want to go with *him* to the tango contest. (*Him* is in the objective case because it is the object of the preposition *with*.)

■ **Possessive case.** A pronoun is in the possessive case when it shows possession. It always answers the question "Whose?"

Inga and Dimitri have *their* own way of dancing the tango. (*Their* is in the possessive case because it is the possessive modifier of *own way*.)

Special consideration. The case of a pronoun is independent of its antecedent. Three pronouns in the same sentence can share the same antecedent but still play different roles in the sentence, as in:

Dimitri wants to make sure that when *he* [subject] arrives next week someone will be at the station to meet *him* [object] and to help carry *his* [possessive] luggage. (All three pronouns have the same antecedent—Dimitri—but each plays a different role in the sentence.)

The table that follows illustrates the various forms of personal pronouns, based on their case.

Personal Pronoun Forms Based on Their Case

	Subjective	Objective	Possessive
1st person singular	I	me	my/mine
2nd person singular	you	you	your/yours
3rd person singular (masc.)	he	him	his
3rd person singular (fem.)	she	her	her/hers
1st person plural	we	us	our/ours
2nd person plural	you	you	your/yours
3rd person plural	they	them	their/theirs

Tough Calls

A look at the pronoun errors that occur the most frequently

ANTECEDENT ANXIETY: Mistaken identities

Guideline. Make doubly sure the connection between any PRONOUN and its ANTECEDENT is unmistakable.

A closer look. Most readers will automatically connect a pronoun with the noun or pronoun that immediately pre-

cedes it in the sentence—whether that noun or pronoun
is the antecedent or not. To make sure this reflex doesn't
produce confusion, look to see that the pronoun and its
antecedent are *not* separated by a word or words that
could conceivably be mistaken for the antecedent.

> Dimitri's father joined the Foreign Legion when <u>he</u> was
> three years old. (The connection between the pronoun <u>he</u>
> and its antecedent is vague enough to create the impres-
> sion—initially at least—that Dimitri's father was the
> youngest person ever to join the Foreign Legion.)

Better:

> When Dimitri was three years old, his father joined the
> Foreign Legion.

BETTER THAN I or BETTER THAN ME: Unfinished business

Guideline. Pronouns at the tail end of a comparison take
the same CASE form as the noun or pronoun that is doing
the comparing, or is being compared to.

A closer look. A good way to apply this guideline is to
finish off the sentence by repeating the original verb
mentally. Doing so will usually tell you whether the
pronoun is the SUBJECT or the OBJECT of a VERB.

> Calpurnia does the tango much better than <u>I</u>. (The pro-
> noun is in the subjective case because the word it is being
> compared to—*Calpurnia*—is the subject of the verb <u>does</u>.
> Test: "Calpurnia does the tango better than <u>I</u> [do the
> tango].")

> If I had to make a choice today, I would choose Nero
> rather than <u>him</u>. (The pronoun is in the objective case

because the word it is being compared to—Nero—is the object of the verb _choose_. Test: "If I had to make a choice today, I would choose Nero rather than [choose] _him_.")

BETWEEN YOU AND I or
BETWEEN YOU AND ME: Compound mistake

Guideline. Don't be confused by pronouns that are part of compound constructions.

A closer look. A compound construction is one in which two or more words share the same role in a sentence. When a pronoun is the final element in these constructions, there's a tendency to use the wrong form, particularly when the choice is between _I_ and _me_. A good way to tell which form is correct in these situations is to see how the sentence would sound if that pronoun were by itself, or if it were the _first_ word in the construction.

I am hoping that we will be able to keep this discussion about the tango contest between you and _me_. (Both _you_ and _me_ are OBJECTS of the preposition _between_. Test: You wouldn't say ". . . . to keep this discussion about the tango contest between _I_ and _you_.")

It was nice of you to invite Inga and _me_ to your party next week. (Both _Inga_ and _me_ are OBJECTS of the verbal phrase _to invite_, which puts the pronoun in the objective case. Test: You wouldn't say, "It was nice of you to invite _I_ to your party next week.")

Leonora and I were hoping that you would join _her_ and _me_ at the Gypsy conference next week. (_Leonora_ and _I_ are both SUBJECTS of the verb _were hoping; her_ and _me_ are both OBJECTS of the verb _join_. Test: You wouldn't say, "_Me_ and Leonora were hoping that you would join _she_ and _I_.")

IT IS I or IT IS ME: Linking up

Guideline. Favor the SUBJECTIVE CASE form for pronouns that follow LINKING VERBS, but don't force the issue in conversation.

> It was _they_ who initiated the idea of holding the tango contest in Bratislava next year. (_They_ is in the subjective case because it follows the linking verb _was_.)

> It is _we_ who must take the responsibility for the problems that occurred when we called for all the king's horses. (_We_ is in the subjective case because it follows the linking verb _is_.)

But:

> If anyone can vouch for Dimitri's dependability, it's _me_. (_I_ is technically correct, but _me_ is the natural choice in conversation and is considered acceptable in all but the most formal writing situations.)

MYSELF or ME: Beware of self-indulgence

Guideline. Confine your use of pronouns ending in -_self_ to those situations in which the -_self_ forms are appropriate. Don't fall victim to the misguided assumption that "myself" is a more elegant way of saying "I" or "me."

> Inga and _I_ would love to judge this year's tango contest. (There is no need for _myself_; _I_ is the proper choice.)

> We would like to invite Calpurnia and _you_ to travel with us next spring to Bratislava. (There is no need for _yourself_; _you_ is the proper choice.)

A closer look. There are two legitimate uses of pronouns

that end in -*self*. One is for emphasis. The other is with
REFLEXIVE VERBS.

■ Emphasis

I *myself* will be handling the arrangements for the coronation. (Following *I* with *myself* emphasizes that the speaker intends to take full responsibility for the arrangements.)

Juno *herself* will write the acceptance speech. (No speech writers need apply for the job.)

■ Reflexive Verbs

The children amused *themselves* by reading poetry and by pouring sand down the sink. (*Themselves* is the object of *amused* [a reflexive verb] and refers back to *children.*)

Lucius has a habit of talking to *himself* whenever he is shaving the emperor. (*Himself* is the object of the preposition *to,* and refers back to Lucius.)

Possible exception:

As for *myself*, the plans for the Bratislava trip are still up in the air. (*Me* is probably the better choice, but *myself* could be defended on the grounds that the writer or speaker wants to emphasize the first person pronoun and has elected to omit *me.*)

WHO, WHICH, or THAT: Relative calm

Guideline. Use *that* to introduce RELATIVE CLAUSES that are RESTRICTIVE, and *which* to introduce relative clauses that are NONRESTRICTIVE. Use *who* for both restrictive and nonrestrictive clauses in which the ANTE-

CEDENT is a person. (For more on restrictive and non-restrictive clauses, see pages 18 and 162.)

> We are looking for ice cream flavors *that* will generate a lot of excitement and controversy. (*That* is the proper choice because the clause it introduces is restrictive; it limits the meaning of *ice cream flavors* to only those flavors that *will generate a lot of excitement and controversy*.)

> We will now turn our attention to my favorite five ice cream flavors, *which* we have looked at in great detail over the past two weeks. (*Which* is the proper choice because the clause it introduces is nonrestrictive. Even without *which we have looked at in great detail over the past two weeks,* readers would still know which ice cream flavors were being referred to.)

> The dinner *that* I attended last night was held in honor of my Uncle Ned. (*That* is the proper choice because the clause it introduces is restrictive: It limits the meaning of *dinner* to one dinner only—the one *that I attended last night*. Without this clause, the reader wouldn't know which dinner was being talked about.)

> Last night's dinner, *which* was held in honor of my Uncle Ned, lasted until midnight. (*Which* is the proper choice because the clause it introduces is nonrestrictive. Even without the clause *which was held in honor of my Uncle Ned*, the reader would still know which dinner the writer was referring to.)

But:

> The man *who* came to dinner last night was my Uncle Ned. (*Who* is the proper choice because the antecedent is a person—the *man*.)

> My sister Eileen, *who* lives in Boston, is a terrific tango dancer. (*Who* is the proper choice because its antecedent is a person—*Eileen*.)

A closer look. Here are two situations in which you can safely bend the previous principles.

■ When you are referring to a *category* of people, as opposed to an individual, *that* is frequently a better choice than *who*.

> Socrates was the type of philosopher *that* always asks questions for which no one seems to have the correct answers. (*Type of philosopher* represents a category of people, not an actual person.)

> But:

> Socrates was someone *who* was always asking questions for which no one ever seemed to have the correct answers. (Here the pronoun clearly refers to *Socrates* as a person, not as a type.)

■ *Which* is sometimes a better choice than *that* in a restrictive clause when there are two restrictive clauses in a row and you don't want to repeat *that*.

> I was hoping that any suggestions *which* pertain to next week's Gypsy conference would have been on my desk by now. (Repeating *that* would sound awkward.)

ME TALKING or MY TALKING: Owning up

Guideline. Use the possessive case form of a pronoun that precedes a GERUND.

> *My* coming [not *me coming*] here today to discuss these ice cream flavor ideas was not my idea. (*Coming* is a gerund that operates as the subject of the verb *was*. *My*, therefore, is in the possessive case.)

> We appreciate *your* listening so patiently to our story. (*Listening* is a gerund operating in this sentence as the object of *appreciate*. *Your*, as the modifier, is in the possessive case.)

A closer look. A VERBAL ending in *-ing* isn't always a GERUND. It can sometimes be a PARTICIPLE that modifies a pronoun. In these situations, the pronoun is usually in the objective case. The distinction is one of emphasis: If the emphasis is on the action, use the possessive form. If the emphasis is on the pronoun more than the action, use the objective form.

> I hope you didn't mind *me* interrupting your conversation. (*Me* would be the proper choice here, assuming the emphasis was on the pronoun and not on *interrupting*.)

> I could hear *them* arguing even though I was three tents away from them. (The emphasis is on *them* and not on *arguing*.)

As opposed to:

> I could hear *their* arguing even though I was three tents away from them. (The emphasis is on *arguing*.)

WHO or WHOM: Who cares?

Guideline. Use *who* in all subjective case situations. Use *whom* only when it immediately follows a VERB or PREPOSITION. Be especially careful about using *whom* where it clearly doesn't belong.

> *Who* is coming to dinner tonight? (*Who* is the subject of *is coming*.)

> To *whom* do we owe this honor? (*Whom* is the object of the preposition *to*.)

Who shall I say is calling? (_Who_ is the subject of _is calling_.)

We want this message read by everyone _who_ has ever spoken to Socrates. (_Who_ is the subject of _has spoken_.)

A closer look. Using _who_ instead of _whom_ at the beginning of a question, as in "_Who_ did you speak to?" is considered acceptable English by most authorities, but _whom_ is still the preferred choice immediately after a verb or preposition. The exception: when it is also the subject of a verb.

We should give the assignment to _whoever_ wants it. (Even though _whoever_ follows _to_, a preposition, it is nonetheless the subject of _wants_.)

I would like to introduce you to my friends, Dimitri and Inga, _who_, I believe, have already spoken to you. (The pronoun is the subject of _have spoken_.)

HIS; HIS OR HER; or THEIR: Sex and the singular pronoun

Guideline. Do your best to avoid or to work around any situation that obliges you to choose from _he_, _she_, or _their_ when the gender of a singular antecedent could be either masculine or feminine.

A closer look. Gender agreement as it applies to third-person indefinite pronouns (_anybody, somebody, nobody,_ etc.) is not only a grammatical issue but a social and legal issue as well. The problem is that English doesn't have an all-purpose, gender-inclusive third-person singular equivalent to _their_—a singular pronoun that can be used in reference to either a man or a woman. So, if you are obliged to use *he* or *she* or *him* or *her*, you have the following options:

1. Use *he* (or its equivalent) in all situations when gender is open to question.

> If anybody knows where Inga is, I want <u>him</u> to call me immediately.

> We are looking for somebody who wants to volunteer <u>his</u> services at next year's tango contest.

Comment. Using the masculine third-person pronoun as a gender-inclusive pronoun is the traditional grammar rule. It was established 300 years ago and received official sanction in England through an Act of Parliament in 1850. The rule still prevails in most publishing houses, magazines, and newspaper style books, but is considered inappropriate in many circles and is specifically banned in many organizations. If you use it, be prepared to defend yourself.

2. Use *he or she* or *he/she*.

> If anybody knows where Inga is, I want <u>him or her</u> to call me immediately.

> We are looking for somebody who wants to volunteer <u>his/her</u> services at next year's tango contest.

Comment. This is a safe option, but it can be awkward to use, especially in conversation.

3. Use *them* or *their*.

> If anybody knows where Inga is, I want <u>them</u> to call me immediately.

We are looking for somebody who wants to volunteer _their_ services at next year's tango contest.

Comment. This option violates one of the most hallowed principles of grammar—that singular antecedents demand the singular form of the pronoun. On the other hand, it is politically safe and probably the best option to use in conversation, if not in writing.

4. Rewrite to eliminate *he* or *she* altogether.

If anybody knows where Inga is, I want a call immediately. (The sentence has been rewritten to eliminate the need for a second pronoun.)

We are looking for a volunteer to judge this year's tango contest. (The sentence has been rewritten to eliminate the need for a second pronoun.)

Comment. This option is acceptable politically and grammatically, but not always easy to do.

5. Replace the indefinite pronoun with a plural noun.

If any of the staff members know where Inga is, I want _them_ to call me immediately. (Making the antecedent plural enables us to use _them_ rather than _he_ or _she_.)

We are looking for people [plural] who want [plural] to volunteer _their_ services at next year's tango contest.

Comment. This is probably the best option to use, assuming you can use the plural without butchering the sentence.

CHAPTER 3

Coming to Agreement

Getting subjects and verbs to agree

Adhering to the principle of subject and verb agreement is a lot like brushing your teeth—you don't have to consult a guidebook every time you do it. Most of us do not need a dictionary to tell us that "I *are* coming" or "they *am* going" is incorrect English. And even without the aid of a computerized grammar checker, most of us are able to navigate with ease the quirky fact that while most nouns form their plurals by *adding s*, it is the *dropping* of the *s* that converts the third-person-singular form of most verbs to the plural form. One dog barks. Two dogs bark.

Why, then, devote a chapter to subject and verb agreement? Simply because in many situations this normally straightforward principle can become fiendishly complicated. This chapter will give you a glimpse of these situations and will offer some advice on how to work your way through them without driving yourself crazy.

An Overview

The basic principle of SUBJECT and VERB agreement is this: When the subject of a verb is singular, the verb should be expressed in its singular form. When the subject of the verb is plural, the verb should be expressed in its plural form. Stop on red. Go on green. Now for the fine print:

■ Agreement and Sentence Structure

The subject of a verb is always a NOUN, a PRONOUN, or a PHRASE, but it is not necessarily the noun, pronoun, or phrase that immediately *precedes* the verb in the sentence. Consider the following example:

> The book that described the many wonderful dinners we have shared at Nero's parties was fun to read.

Run this sentence through the typical computerized grammar checker and you will probably be advised to change *was* to *were*. That's because grammar checkers, not yet sophisticated enough to read the mind of the person who composed the sentence, are programmed to match the number of the verb with the number of the noun or pronoun that immediately *precedes* the verb in the sentence.

As it happens, the subject of the verb in most cases is indeed the noun or pronoun that immediately precedes the verb. But you can write a respectable sentence in which a noun or pronoun other than the true subject immediately precedes the verb. The subject of the verb in the preceding example, for instance, is *book*, a singular noun.

The message here: Keep in mind that except for a handful of situations, *how* a sentence is constructed has no bearing on the numerical relationship between the subject and its verb. If the subject is singular, it doesn't matter where the subject is positioned in the sentence with respect to the verb; the verb is singular as well.

■ Notional Agreement

Notional agreement means that in some subject and verb situations the verb can be either singular or plural, depending upon your notion—depending, that is, on the number of people or items your subject is meant to represent.

Most of the time, of course, the number of people or items represented by the subject is obvious. But with certain types of nouns and pronouns—words like *team*, *group*, *committee*, *any*, and *none*—the verb can be either singular or plural, depending on how you view the noun or pronoun: as a single unit or as a number of people or things acting separately. The word *team*, for instance, usually operates as a singular noun, as in:

The team *is* holding a meeting tomorrow morning.

If, however, your sentence refers to actions being taken by individual members of the team, the word might be considered a plural, as in:

The team performed well today and _have_ [plural] every right to hold their heads high.

The nice thing about notional agreement is that you can usually defend any choice you make. The risky thing is that people less enlightened than you might not be aware that, having read this book, you recognize _both_ possibilities, singular or plural, and have deliberately chosen one over the other because . . . well, you get the picture.

Disagreeable Situations

A look at those agreement situations that create special problems

ANY, ANY ONE, ANYONE, or ANYBODY: Anything goes

Guideline. Use a singular VERB when its subject is _any one_, _anyone_, or _anybody_. Let the number of the NOUN that follows _any_ determine the number of the verb.

Does [singular] _anybody_ know a good tango orchestra? (The verb is singular because _anybody_ refers to one person.)

Does [singular] _anyone_ who saw the egg fall off the wall know how it happened? (The verb is singular because _anyone_ always takes a singular verb.)

_Do_ [plural] _any_ of the people who saw the egg fall off the wall _know_ how it happened? (_Do_ and _know_ are plural because their number is governed by _people,_ a plural noun.)

COLLECTIVE NOUNS: Majority rule

Guideline. Use the singular form of a VERB following most COLLECTIVE NOUNS—nouns that represent a group of persons or things that usually operate as a unit. But use the plural form when the verb expresses actions being taken by individual members of that unit. (See box, p. 68.)

A team of investigators _is_ arriving from Carthage tomorrow. (The verb is singular because the members of the team will be arriving as a unit.)

The orchestra _sounds_ better today than ever, especially since we have changed tuba players. (_Orchestra_ takes a singular verb because it is being considered as a unit.)

But:

The orchestra _are_ rehearsing today in different rooms. (_Orchestra_ takes the plural form of the verb because the assumption here is that individual members of the orchestra are working independently.)

COMPOUND SUBJECTS JOINED BY _AND:_ Compound interest

Guideline. Use the plural form of the VERB when two SUBJECTS share the same verb and are joined by _and._ The exception: when the two subjects joined by _and_ are normally thought of as a single unit.

A fool and his gold *are* soon parted. (Two singular subjects—*fool* and *gold*—form a compound subject joined by *and.* They require the plural form of the verb.)

Romeo and Juliet [separate entities] are interesting characters, but love and marriage is not my favorite subject.

Collective Wisdom

Applying the principle of agreement to collective nouns is a minefield for people who like their grammar principles nicely buttoned down. The main problem is that what is technically correct often *sounds* wrong. That's because Americans (more so than the English) are accustomed to associating singular-sounding nouns with the singular form of the verb. It is technically correct, for instance, to say, "The team usually *do* their best when they are behind," but most educated Americans are uncomfortable with the use of *do* in this instance.

The best approach: Decide whether you want the collective noun to be considered as a unit or as a group of individuals acting separately, and make the appropriate verb choice. If the sentence still sounds funny, see if you can find a plural noun to insert (i.e., team *members* instead of team; staff *members* instead of staff, etc.).

Our team members *do* their best to follow the rules, but they're only a bunch of gladiators. (Changing *team* to *team members* eliminates the problem of having to choose between the singular [*does*] and the plural [*do*].)

The crew members *are* going to be arriving from Carthage at different times. (Again, adding *members* automatically makes the verb plural.)

COMPOUND SUBJECTS CONNECTED BY *OR:* When less is more

Guideline. Use the singular form of the VERB when two or more SUBJECTS are connected by *or*—with the following exceptions: (1) when *all* the subjects are plural; (2) when the subject *nearest* the verb is plural.

> Either Jack or Jill *is* going to be with us on the climb tomorrow morning. (The verb is singular because both subjects joined by *or*—*Jack* and *Jill*—are singular.)

> Either the Democrats or the Republicans *are* going to be with us on the climb. (The verb is plural because both subjects—*Democrats* and *Republicans* joined by *or*—are plural.)

> Either Jack or the Republicans *are* going to be with us on the climb. (The verb is plural because *Republicans*, the subject closest to the verb, is plural.)

> Either the Republicans or Jack *is* going to be with us on the climb. (The verb is singular because *Jack*, the subject closest to the verb, is singular.)

A closer look. When the NOUNS or PRONOUNS that make up a COMPOUND SUBJECT represent different PERSONS (first person [I], second person [you], etc.), the form of the VERB is governed by the person of the word *nearest* the verb.

> Either Inga or I *am* going to judge the tango contest. (The choice of *am* over *is* is governed by the fact that *I* [first person: *am*] is closer to the verb than *Inga* [third person: *is*].)

COMPOUND SUBJECTS WITH *NEITHER/NOR:* Two-way street

Guideline. Follow the same guidelines that govern subjects connected by *or.*

> Neither Jack nor Jill *has* any interest in climbing that hill anymore. (The verb is singular because *Jack* and *Jill* are both singular.)

> Neither the Democrats nor the Republicans *have* any interest in climbing the hill. (The verb is plural because *Democrats* and *Republicans* are both plural.)

> Neither the Democrats nor Jill *has* any interest in climbing the hill. (The verb is singular because *Jill,* a singular noun, is closer to the verb than *Democrats.*)

> Neither Jack nor the Republicans *have* any interest in climbing the hill. (The verb is plural because *Republicans,* a plural noun, is closer to the verb than *Jack.*)

EACH OF: Judgment call

Guideline. Use the singular form of the VERB most of the time, but not when you want to emphasize the plural NOUN that follows *of.*

A closer look. The best way to determine the form of the verb followed by *each* is to insert the word *one* to see how it affects your meaning and emphasis. If you want a different emphasis, use the plural form.

> *Each of* the tango contest entries *is* competing for the first time. (The emphasis here is on each individual entry.)

> *Each of* the entries *are* to be judged on their own merit. (The emphasis here is on *all* of the contestants, besides

which the presence of *their*, a plural pronoun, dictates the plural form of the verb.)

Each of us *is* [or *are*] responsible for what happened after the king's horses left the scene. (Either choice is proper, depending upon where you want the emphasis: on people individually [singular] or on all the members of the group [plural].)

EITHER OF or NEITHER OF: Lone Rangers

Guideline. Use the singular form of the VERB in PHRASES or CLAUSES that begin with *either of* or *neither of*, regardless of the number of the NOUN that follows.

I don't care which of the two people I dance with. *Either of* them *is* fine with me. (*Either of* constructions require the singular form of the verb.)

Neither of the senators I spoke to last night *wants* to have anything to do with Cassius. (*Neither of* constructions require the singular form of the verb.)

MONEY MATTERS: Unit costs

Guideline. Use the singular form of the VERB when a specific sum of money is mentioned. Use the plural form when the reference is to an indefinite number.

Twenty dollars *is* a lot of money to spend on a left-handed screwdriver. (The verb is singular because *twenty dollars* is expressed as a single unit.)

Thousands of dollars *have been* spent on the Lunar Tides and Productivity Project. (The verb is plural because *thousands of dollars* represents an indefinite number.)

NEGATIVE CONSTRUCTIONS: Singular no's

Guideline. Use the singular form of the VERB when a SUBJECT is followed by a negative PHRASE. The exception: when the subject is plural.

> Jack and not Jill _is_ going to climb the hill. (The verb is singular because _Jack_ is a singular subject followed by a negative construction.)

> Jack and not the Republicans _is_ going to climb the hill tomorrow. (The verb remains singular even though _Republicans_ is plural and even though it is closer to the verb than _Jack_: _Jack_ is still the subject.)

> Good feelings and not a physical workout _are_ our main concerns with this morning's climb. (The verb is plural because its subject is _feelings_.)

NONE: More than meets the eye

Guideline. Base your choice on whether you want _none_ to mean "not one" (singular) or "not any" (plural).

A closer look. The universal view among grammarians today is that _none_ can be either singular or plural, depending on the intended meaning of the sentence.

The most sensible approach is this: If the noun that follows _of_ in a phrase introduced by _none_ is singular, make the verb singular. If the noun is plural, base your choice on whether you would be more inclined to use _not one_ (singular) or _not any_ (plural) after _none_.

> None of the money _has_ been spent. (The verb is singular because the noun following _none_ [_money_] is singular.)

None of the jobs *have* [or *has*] been completed yet. (The choice here hinges on whether the intended meaning of the sentence is better served by *not one* of the jobs [singular] or *not any* of the jobs [plural].)

None of the tango dancers *has* arrived yet. (Intended meaning: *Not one* of the tango dancers *has* arrived yet.)

None of the tango dancers have arrived yet. (Intended meaning: *Not any* of the dancers have arrived.)

NOUNS ENDING IN "S": False impression

Guideline. Use the singular form of the VERB for NOUNS ending in *s*, except when the noun refers to a plural idea.

The news about Dimitri *is* good. (The verb is singular because *news* refers to one thing.)

Economics *has* always been a key factor in our tango contest decisions. (The verb is singular because *economics* refers to a single subject.)

The economics of the situation *are* such that we have to introduce the new flavor next month. (The verb is plural because *economics* refers to a number of different factors.)

NOUN PLURALS THAT DON'T END IN "S": No change

Guideline. Treat NOUNS whose plurals do not end in *s* the same way you would treat normal plurals.

The alumni *are* scheduled to arrive at noon.

The criteria we *are* establishing will help ensure the quality of our flavor development process.

ONE OF THOSE ... WHO or THAT: Splitting hairs

Guideline. Base the form of the VERB that follows *one of those . . . who* or *one of those . . . that* constructions on where you want to place the emphasis: on the *one* in *one of* or on the word that precedes the pronoun.

A closer look. Here is one of the thorniest issues in grammar—and one of those principles (speaking of *one of those* constructions) that can be argued both ways.

The key question is which word do you want to serve as the antecedent for *who: one*, or the word that immediately precedes *who?* Since either of the two words can usually qualify, it's up to you to make the choice, based on the emphasis you want to give to each word. Look at the following examples:

> Hamlet is <u>one</u> of those persons <u>who likes</u> to get involved with every decision. (Expressing <u>likes</u> in the singular form puts more emphasis on <u>one</u> than on <u>persons</u>.)

But:

> Hamlet is one of those <u>persons who like</u> to get involved with every decision. (<u>Like</u>, the plural form, gives more emphasis to <u>persons</u> than to <u>one</u>.)

Another but:

> Ophelia is <u>one</u> of those <u>persons who likes</u> to do things her own way. (The use of the singular pronoun <u>her</u> makes <u>likes</u> [singular] the better choice, regardless of emphasis.)

> Ophelia is one of those <u>persons who like</u> to do things their own way. (The use of the plural pronoun <u>their</u> makes <u>like</u> [plural] the better choice.)

PARENTHETICAL PHRASES AND CLAUSES: No effect

Guideline. Do not allow PARENTHETICAL PHRASES or CLAUSES to influence your choice of a singular or plural VERB.

> The new employee hot tub, along with the six astrologers we have hired, _has_ already begun to improve morale. (_Along with the six astrologers we have hired_ is a parenthetical clause and not technically part of the subject, _hot tub_.)

> The six new astrologers, along with the new employee hot tub, _have_ combined to improve employee morale. (The subject of the verb _have combined_ is now _astrologers_.)

PERCENTAGE DECISIONS: Numbers' crunch

Guideline. Base your choice in most cases on the number of the NOUN that immediately precedes the VERB.

> Roughly 50 percent of the pyramid _is_ now complete. (The verb is singular because _pyramid_ is singular.)

> Roughly 50 percent of the tango dancers _were_ clearly unprepared for the trip to Bratislava. (The verb is plural because _tango dancers_ is plural.)

PHRASES AND CLAUSES AS SUBJECTS: Ganging up

Guideline. Use a singular VERB when the SUBJECT of a verb is a PHRASE or CLAUSE, no matter how many people or things are mentioned in the phrase or clause.

> Getting all the invitations mailed in time for the Ides of March _is_ costing us more than we thought it would. (The

subject of this sentence is the phrase *Getting all the invitations mailed in time for the Ides of March*.)

THERE IS or THERE ARE: Afterthoughts

Guideline. Base the number of any VERB following *there* on the number represented by the NOUN or PRONOUN that follows.

There *is* one thing I want to emphasize about our decision to cancel the Lunar Tides and Productivity Project. (The verb is singular because *thing* is singular.)

There *are* two points I want to emphasize about our decision to resume the Lunar Tides and Productivity Project. (The verb is plural because *points* is plural.)

A closer look. The contraction *there's* applies only to *there is* and not *there are*. There is no contraction for *there are*. *They're* is the contraction for *they are*.

CHAPTER 4

End Games

How to tame vicious verbs

Verbs are tough to get your arms around in any language, and the verbs in English are no exception.

Apart from being the most important part of speech—you can't form a thought without one—the verb is the most chameleon-like creature in grammar. Its forms (endings mostly) are forever changing. They change to reflect the TENSE of the verb (the time frame it refers to). They change to reflect the PERSON and

NUMBER of the verb's SUBJECT. They even change in certain situations to reflect the intention behind the sentence: whether it's a simple statement or an expression of doubt, desire, or conjecture.

These myriad changes notwithstanding, verbs in English are not nearly as demonic to deal with as the verbs in certain languages (Greek, for instance) in which the number of individual verb forms could easily fill the *Yellow Pages*. The changes most English verbs undergo are relatively slight and strikingly uniform. And even when you are dealing with the so-called irregular verbs (see pages 79–85), English rarely obliges you to memorize more than three or four forms.

I have made no attempt in this chapter to cover every aspect of verb usage. I assume that you understand the differences between the various TENSES (present, past, future, etc.) and that you understand the concepts of person and number as they relate to verbs. Given these assumptions, I will be focusing in this chapter on those specific verb-related areas that create the most mischief for most people.

Happy Endings

An overview of verb forms

All verb forms, regardless of the situation, are built around three basic forms, known as the PRINCIPAL PARTS of a verb. These are the forms that are normally used when you express the verb in the first person of the PRESENT TENSE, the PAST TENSE, or the PRESENT PERFECT, usually referred to as the PARTICIPLE.

Sometimes you have to modify one of these basic forms: add an *s*, perhaps, or an *ing*, or, in the case of the PERFECT TENSES, precede the verb with either *have* or *had*. Essentially, though, if you know the principal parts of a verb, you know every form the verb could possibly assume. Your only problem now is deciding which of the three forms (with minor modifications) is appropriate in the various situations that call for a different verb form.

Regular vs. Irregular

Depending upon how they form their principal parts, verbs are often divided into two categories: regular and irregular. Regular verbs form their principal parts in the simplest of ways: by adding *-ed* to the root form in both the past and present perfect forms. Irregular verbs, however, follow no set pattern.

The good news is that there are far more regular verbs in English than there are irregular verbs. The bad news is that irregular verbs include the verbs we use the most frequently.

Here is a look at both categories and their principal parts:

Regular Verbs

Present	Past	Past participle (have or had:)
call	called	called
dance	danced	danced
elope	eloped	eloped
mingle	mingled	mingled

Irregular Verbs

What follows are examples of the verbs that are frequently mishandled. The three forms listed are the present, the past, and the participle. Notice that when any form of the verb *have* precedes the main verb, the correct form is always the participle. (Note: A comprehensive list of irregular verbs and their principal parts appears on pages 82–85.)

ARISE, AROSE, ARISEN

A serious problem *has arisen* [not *has arose*], and we would like you to return from Bratislava as soon as possible.

BEGIN, BEGAN, BEGUN

We could *have begun* [not *have began*] the meeting sooner if the discussion of new ice cream flavors had not dragged on for such a long time.

BEND, BENT, BENT

We *have bent* [not *have bended*] over backward to accommodate Dimitri's requests.

CAST, CAST, CAST

We *have cast* [not *have casted*] aside our old ideas about developing ice cream flavors.

DO, DID, DONE

There isn't much anybody could *have done* [not could *have did*] to prevent the egg from falling off the wall.

GET, GOT, GOT (OR GOTTEN)

Have you *got* [or *gotten*] everything you need for next week's tango contest?

GO, WENT, GONE

We would not *have gone* [not would not *have went*] to the meeting if we had known there was going to be a tango contest.

LAY, LAID, LAID
Since the accident near the wall, the king *has laid* [not *has layed*] down some strict laws about egg usage.

LIE, LAY, LAIN
Yesterday, after I came home from the tango contest, I *lay* [not *layed* or *laid*] down for several hours on the couch in my office.

PROVE, PROVED, PROVED (or PROVEN)
We *have proved* [or *proven*] beyond doubt that there is a future for the tango.

RUN, RAN, RUN
We could *have run* [not could *have ran*] the tango contest a lot better if there had been more money to spend for the orchestra.

SEE, SAW, SEEN
I can't remember the last time I *saw* [not *seen*] Inga dance so beautifully.

SWEAR, SWORE, SWORN
I could *have sworn* [not could *have swore*] I saw Dimitri last week in Bratislava.

SWIM, SWAM, SWUM
I *swam* [not *swum*] farther today than I *have* ever *swum* [not *swam*].

Irregular Verbs: Most of the Family Tree

Present	Past	Past Participle
arise	arose	arisen
awake	awoke	awaked
	awaked	awoken
bear	bore	borne
beat	beat	beaten/beat
begin	began	begun
bend	bent	bent
bid (offer)	bid	bid
bid (direct address)	bade	bidden
bind	bound	bound
bite	bit	bitten/bit
blow	blew	blown
break	broke	broken
bring	brought	brought
build	built	built
buy	bought	bought
cast	cast	cast
catch	caught	caught
choose	chose	chosen
come	came	come
creep	crept	crept
deal	dealt	dealt
dive	dived/dove	dived
do	did	done
draw	drew	drawn

Present	Past	Past Participle
drink	drank	drunk
drive	drove	driven
eat	ate	eaten
fall	fell	fallen
feed	fed	fed
fight	fought	fought
find	found	found
fling	flung	flung
fly	flew	flown
forbid	forbade	forbidden
forget	forgot	forgotten/forgot
forgive	forgave	forgiven
freeze	froze	frozen
get	got	got/gotten
give	gave	given
go	went	gone
grow	grew	grown
hang [execute]	hanged	hanged
hang [suspend]	hung	hung
has (have)	had	had
hit	hit	hit
hold	held	held
hurt	hurt	hurt
know	knew	known
lay	laid	laid
lead	led	led
leave	left	left
lend	lent	lent

Present	Past	Past Participle
let	let	let
lie	lay	lain
lose	lost	lost
make	made	made
meet	met	met
prove	proved	proved/proven
put	put	put
read	read	read
ride	rode	ridden
ring	rang	rung
rise	rose	risen
run	ran	run
see	saw	seen
seek	sought	sought
sell	sold	sold
send	sent	sent
set	set	set
shine	shone	shone
shrink	shrank/shrunk	shrunken
sing	sang	sung
sink	sank	sunk
slay	slew	slain
sit	sat	sat
sleep	slept	slept
slide	slid	slid
speak	spoke	spoken
spring	sprang/sprung	sprung
steal	stole	stolen
stick	stuck	stuck
sting	stung	stung
strike	struck	struck

Present	Past	Past Participle
swear	swore	sworn
sweat	sweat/sweated	sweated
swim	swam	swum
swing	swung	swung
take	took	taken
teach	taught	taught
tear	tore	torn
tell	told	told
think	thought	thought
throw	threw	thrown
wake	woke/waked	woken/waked

Verbs at Work

Guidelines on how to use verbs more effectively

ACTIVE OR PASSIVE VOICE: Giving or receiving

Guideline. Unless you have a good reason for doing otherwise, express verbs in the ACTIVE rather than the PASSIVE VOICE.

A closer look. A verb is in the *active voice* when its subject is also the performer of the action. It is in the *passive voice* when its subject is something or someone *other* than the doer of the action. While there is nothing grammatically wrong with either construction, expressing verbs in the active rather than the passive voice usually produces sentences that are smoother and more concise. (See box, page 86.)

Active or Passive Voice: Choosing Sides

Its drawbacks notwithstanding, the passive voice has several legitimate—and even preferable—uses. When a verb is expressed in the passive voice (as we've just done), the emphasis shifts from the doer of the action to the object of the action. Here are three reasons you might want this shift to occur:.

■ **Emphasis.** Use the passive voice when the intent of your sentence is better served by giving more emphasis to the receiver of the action than to the doer of the action.

> The plan to relocate the employee hot tub to the warehouse *was met* with stiff opposition. (In this sentence, the *plan* and the fact that it *met with stiff opposition* are more important than the identity of the people opposing it.)

> I will *not be ignored*. (Whoever might be doing the ignoring in this situation is less important than the person who doesn't want to be ignored.)

■ **Tact.** Use the passive voice to soften the impact of a rejection.

> It *was felt* [rather than we *felt*] that your proposal did not sufficiently meet our needs. (Not mentioning the doer of the action takes some of the sting away from the rejection.)

■ **Convenience.** Use the passive voice when you want to avoid using "you."

> The form *is to be filed* immediately. (The passive voice is used here to avoid the use of *you*, as in "*You should file* the form immediately.")

The emperor _called_ our office today while you were at the baths. (_Called_ is in the active voice because its subject, _emperor_, is the doer of the action.)

Our office _was called_ this morning by the emperor. (_Was called_ is in the passive voice because its subject, _our office_, did not perform the action. The _emperor_ did.)

DANGLING VERBALS: Time warp

Guideline. Make sure that VERBAL phrases (see the Glossary for more on verbals) connect logically to the words they relate to.

A closer look. Virtually all verbs can be converted into adjectives by adding either _-ed_ or _-ing_ to the root form. These converted verb forms are known as PARTICIPLES and are part of a larger grammatical group known as VERBALS. Participles usually join with other words to form PARTICIPIAL PHRASES and always modify another word in the sentence. As such, their position in the sentence is critical. This means you need to be careful about writing sentences in which the phrases dangle— that is, do not logically connect to the word or words they are meant to modify.

Concerned about developments in Bratislava, the lunch has been called off. (_Concerned about developments in Bratislava_ is dangling because it doesn't relate to _lunch_. The _lunch_ was not "concerned about developments . . .".)

Better:

Concerned about the developments in Bratislava, we canceled the lunch. (The phrase _concerned about the developments in Bratislava_ no longer dangles; it connects directly to _we._)

Or:

We were concerned about the developments in Bratislava and so we canceled the lunch.

TWO PAST ACTIONS IN THE SAME SENTENCE: Proper timing

Guideline. When two VERBS expressing past actions appear in the same sentence, use the PAST PERFECT TENSE (the verb preceded by *had*) to express the *earlier* of the two actions.

A closer look. Using the past perfect tense for one of the two past actions expressed in the same sentence tells the reader which action took place first. This principle applies to both straight statements and hypothetical statements.

I *had intended* [not I *intended*] before I *arrived* this morning to talk about what happened during last night's tango contest. (*Had intended* is in the past perfect tense because the intention was formed before the arrival.)

I *had not realized* [not *did not realize*] before I began looking into the matter how serious Cassius was about the plan. (*Had not realized* is in the past perfect tense because the realization took place before the speaker began looking into the matter.)

If they *had spent* more time on research and less time talking about the constellations, the Lunar Tides and Productivity Project would have gone much more smoothly. (*Had spent*, the past perfect tense, is used here because the *spending* should have taken place before the project started.)

TO BE or TO HAVE BEEN: Another timing question

Guideline. Favor the PERFECT form of the infinitive (to have . . .) when the action expressed in the infinitive took place before the action expressed in the main verb, but use the simpler form if the sentence sounds awkward.

I am grateful *to have had* the opportunity to work with all of you on the Lunar Tides and Productivity Project. (The expression of gratitude was preceded by the action of having worked on the project.)

Or:

I am grateful I *had* the opportunity to work with all of you on the Lunar Tides and Productivity Project. (The meaning stays the same, but this time a true verb [*had*] is used instead of the infinitive.)

But, either:

The problems were supposed *to have been worked out* before we got together again with Cassius. (Correct grammar but somewhat formal.)

Or:

The problems were supposed *to be worked out* before we got together again with Cassius. (Not quite as proper but generally acceptable.)

IF I WERE or IF I WAS: What's really going on?

Guideline. Use *were* (instead of *was*) in statements that are contrary to fact.

A closer look. Statements contrary to fact, especially those that begin with "if," call for a special form of the verb known as the SUBJUNCTIVE (see box on page 91). Some usage authorities argue that there is no longer a need to worry about this distinction, but careful writers and speakers continue to use subjunctive forms in a few situations—and particularly in *if* clauses that express a statement contrary to fact. The main change you need to make in most of these situations is to substitute *were* for *was*.

> If this _were_ [not _was_] a well-run camel caravan, we wouldn't be lost. (The subjunctive form of _to be_ [_were_] is the proper choice because the statement is contrary to fact: The camel caravan is _not_ well run.)

> If I _were_ you, I wouldn't take part in the tango contest. (_Were_ is the proper choice because the statement is contrary to fact.)

> I have often wished that I _were_ more like Dimitri. (_Were_ is the correct choice even though the main verb is in the past tense. The statement is still contrary to fact.)

> I wish I _were_ in Bratislava. (_Were_ is the proper choice because the statement is contrary to fact.)

But:

> If it _was_ raining yesterday in Bratislava, the tango contest was probably called off. (_Was_ is the proper choice here because there is a good chance that it was raining.)

> The only reason I called was to see if Jesse _was_ still in bed. (The verb here is not in the subjunctive mood because the idea following "if" is _not_ contrary to fact. Jesse's being in bed is a distinct possibility.)

The Subjunctive Mood: A Closer Look

The SUBJUNCTIVE mood is one of three moods (the others are the INDICATIVE mood and the IMPERATIVE mood) that can affect the ending of a verb. Understanding the workings of this mood is not as important in English grammar as it is in other languages. That's because the special forms that at one time set the subjunctive mood apart from other moods have largely disappeared from English. Those forms that do change are pretty much confined to the two situations covered in this section: clauses introduced by *if* that are contrary to fact, and clauses that follow verbs or verb phrases expressing a wish, a request, a command, or a recommendation.

BE or IS: Wishful thinking

Guideline. Use the SUBJUNCTIVE form of the verb *to be (be)* in clauses that follow a verb expressing a request, a demand, a recommendation, or necessity.

A closer look. More often than not, the form of the verb called for in clauses that follow verbs expressing a demand, a recommendation, or necessity is no different from the form you would use in simple statements. The main exception involves the verb *to be*, which calls for *be* in most situations. The distinctions are subtle, but the examples below should help you make the proper choice.

> I would like to suggest that this discussion about ice cream flavors _be_ postponed for at least a week. (_Be_ is used because the clause follows a verb phrase [_like to suggest_] that expresses a suggestion.)

It is essential that the Lunar Tides and Productivity Project _be_ completed by next year. (_Be_ is used because the clause follows a verb that helps to express a necessity.)

I recommend that the site of the meeting _be_ changed to Bratislava. (_Be_ is the proper choice because the clause follows a verb that expresses a recommendation.)

CHAPTER 5

Points Well Taken

How to make your mark in punctuation

The way most people handle punctuation today, you would think its role in writing were strictly janitorial: the mopping up you do after you have finished the truly important work of crafting your words into sentences. You would also think, judging from the randomness with which people spread them throughout their sentences, that punctuation marks were the throw pillows of grammar—to be inserted whenever and wherever the spirit moves you.

Not quite. Punctuation involves more than simply mopping up, and it is far from being a random process. Handled properly, punctuation can do more to enhance the clarity and the flow of your writing than you might think. True, proper punctuation is of little value to writing that is infected with faulty organization and clumsy syntax. But if your writing is reasonably sound, knowing how to punctuate can make it better. The chief benefit: Punctuation gives you a way to achieve in your writing some of the effects you routinely produce in conversation whenever you pause, slow down or increase the pace of your delivery, or change volume or pitch because you want to—well, punctuate certain points.

Punctuation: An Overview

You can approach punctuation in one of two ways, each way represented by a different school of thought. Neither approach has an official name, but a good way to differentiate the two is to think of one as the "by the book" approach and the other as the "depends on your meaning" approach.

If you follow the "by the book" approach to punctuation, you base your decisions solely on the *mechanics* of the sentence. You look at a sentence, analyze its anatomy, and then apply the appropriate punctuation principle. The impact of your punctuation decision—how it affects the meaning, the flow, or the emphasis of the sentence—doesn't concern you.

The "depends on what you mean" school of thought is more situation-oriented. You worry less about how the sentence is constructed and more about how the insertion—or omission—of a particular punctuation mark will influence the meaning, the flow, and the emphasis of the sentence.

Both schools of thought are in accord when it comes to routine punctuation decisions: a period at the end of a sentence, a question mark at the end of a question, etc. Where the schools differ mainly is in the use of commas, and there are strong arguments to support either approach—as long as you stay away from extremes.

The "by the book" approach is simpler to manage (assuming you know the rules and understand the basics of grammar), and it's probably the safer of the two approaches. If you follow it too zealously, however, it can produce punctuation decisions that inadvertently obscure or change the meaning behind the sentence.

The "depends on what you mean" approach allows you more latitude, but it also leaves your punctuation decisions more open to attack from those who favor the "by the book" approach. So even if you follow this approach, you still need to understand traditional punctuation principles.

The punctuation philosophy I have chosen to follow in *Grammar for Smart People* is a hybrid of these two general approaches. I have remained faithful to most of the generally accepted principles of punctuation, but when the clarity or flow of a sentence would have been ill-served, I have not felt compelled to follow a principle. In short, I have tried to apply what you should apply whenever you punctuate: common sense.

Putting Commas in Their Place

A summary of the most common uses of the comma

The COMMA (,) has more uses than any other punctuation mark, and for that reason alone it gets *misused* more than any other punctuation mark. It's a simple matter of the law of averages.

The basic function of the comma—and a function it shares to some extent with the SEMICOLON, the DASH, and the COLON—is to create pauses *within* the body of a sentence. These pauses serve one of two purposes: one, they promote clarity; two, they help control the rhythm of the sentence and the emphasis accorded to specific ideas or images.

Summarized in this section are the situations that generally require a comma decision. Before we get to these specific situations, though, here are some observations about comma use in general.

1. **Two-way street.** It is just as bad to insert commas where they don't belong as it is to omit them where they clearly *do* belong.

2. **Two for the road.** Commas that set off elements *within* the body of a sentence almost always come in pairs—one at the beginning of the element and the other at the end. You can frequently defend a decision to leave *both* commas out, but you can rarely defend a decision to use just one comma and leave the other out.

3. **Lean and mean.** The tighter your sentences, the less need for commas. So if you find yourself making an abundance of comma decisions in a single sentence, chances are the sentence is too convoluted. Simplify.

4. **Beyond the law.** If adhering to a comma "rule" could conceivably obscure the meaning of your sentence, ditch the rule.

ITEMS IN A SERIES: Group therapy

Guideline. Use a comma to separate items (words, PHRASES, and CLAUSES) that follow each other in a series but are not separated by a CONJUNCTION. Be consistent when it comes to punctuating the next-to-last item in the series. (See box, page 98.)

> Last night's dinner menu consisted of goose liver, leg of lamb, and dessert. (Commas are needed because _goose liver_, _leg of lamb_, and _dessert_ are items in a series.)

> The noise occurs when we turn the machine on, when we turn it off, and when we move from one speed to the next. (Commas are needed because the three clauses in the sentence appear in a series.)

A closer look. This rule usually applies to a series of _three_ items or more (most series consisting of two items are separated by a conjunction and therefore do not need a comma to keep them distinct). Its main purpose is to prevent the confusion that arises in the following sentences:

> Last night's dinner menu consisted of goose liver leg of lamb and dessert.

> The noise occurs when we turn the machine on when we turn it off and when we move from one speed to the next.

The Comma Before the Final *"and"* in a Series

A look at the options

When it comes to inserting or omitting the comma that precedes the conjunction before the last item—the technical term is the serial comma—no fewer than three options are legitimately open to you. Here are the options, along with the pros and cons of each. You can decide for yourself which rule to adopt.

Option one: *Always* use it before the *and*, no matter how many items are in the series.

Option two: Insert it when you think it's needed; leave it out when you don't think it's needed.

Option three: Omit it when there are only three items in the series, but insert it once the number of items reaches four or above. Exception: when omitting the comma might create ambiguity.

Choosing sides: The first is favored by many publishing houses and by the publishers of scholarly magazines. It's the simplest to follow, and the principle I have used in this book. The second is widely used by newspapers and magazines, whose editors like this option because it saves space. The last of these three options is old-fashioned and isn't followed much anymore.

Whichever option you choose, make sure that clarity doesn't suffer. In other words, *always* insert a comma before the final conjunction if there is any chance that the meaning might be misunderstood because of the comma's absence.

MODIFIERS IN A SERIES: Parallel tracks

Guideline. Use a comma to separate two or more ADJEC-TIVES that modify the same noun, but only when the adjectives represent qualities that are *parallel* to or *independent* of each other.

A closer look. To tell whether adjectives in a series are independent modifiers (and should be separated by commas), see what happens when you insert the word *and* between them. If the insertion produces gibberish, the adjectives need to act as a unit and should *not* be separated by a comma. If the phrase still makes sense with the *and*, use a comma.

> The report offers a *penetrating, accurate* analysis of the frozen guacamole industry. (A comma is needed between *penetrating* and *accurate* because each adjective could act as an independent modifier. Test: . . . a *penetrating and accurate* analysis . . . makes sense.)

> We held the tango contest in the large blue room next to the cafeteria. (No comma is needed between *large* and *blue* because the two modifiers work in tandem to identify the room. Test: . . . a *large and blue room* . . . doesn't make sense.)

RESTRICTIVE AND NONRESTRICTIVE CLAUSES: Life support

Guideline. Base your decision to insert or omit commas before and after RELATIVE CLAUSES on the extent to which the clause limits the meaning of the word it refers back to. Omit commas when the clause is RESTRICTIVE—limits the meaning. Insert commas when the clause is

NONRESTRICTIVE—doesn't limit the meaning. (For more on restrictive and nonrestrictive clauses, see page 162.)

> People *who live in glass houses* shouldn't throw stones. (No commas are needed here because *who live in glass houses* is a restrictive clause. The sentence would not retain its intended meaning if the clause were left out.)

> The people next door, *who live in a glass house,* have begun throwing stones. (Commas are needed here because *who live in a glass house* is nonrestrictive. It isn't necessary to identify who is meant by "the people next door.")

THE APPOSITIVE: Mirror image

Guideline. Use commas to set off any word or words that are APPOSITIVE to another word in the sentence.

A closer look. A word or group of words is in apposition to another word when it is, in effect, a mirror image of that word: when it is the same part of speech and relates to the rest of the sentence in the same way. The most common mistake people make with appositives is to use only one comma—rather than a set.

> James Trout, *the noted fishing expert,* will [not *James Trout, the noted fishing expert* (no comma) *will* . . .] be the guest speaker at next week's clambake. (The phrase in italics is in apposition to the subject.)

> Alligator wrestling, *a sport that originally developed in Florida,* has begun to lose some of its appeal, especially among the alligators. (The clause in italics is in apposition to the subject, *alligator wrestling.*)

An even closer look. Don't confuse a true appositive with a noun preceded by a MODIFIER.

Noted fishing expert James Trout will be the guest speaker at next week's clambake. (No comma is needed here because *Noted fishing expert* is a modifier, not an appositive.)

CLAUSES AND PHRASES THAT INTRODUCE A SENTENCE: Just for openers

Guideline. Use a comma to separate lengthy introductory phrases or dependent clauses from the main body of the sentence. Make an exception for phrases that are short and refer to time and place.

As you requested, I am sending along an autographed photograph of the emperor. (A comma follows *requested* because *as you requested* is an introductory clause that precedes the main body of the sentence.)

Despite the fact that snow is predicted for Friday, we have no plans to cancel the tango contest. (*Despite the fact that snow is predicted for Friday* is followed by a comma because it is an introductory clause preceding the main body of a sentence.)

Having discounted every other possibility, we are now convinced that Dimitri is somewhere in Bratislava. (*Having discounted every other possibility* is followed by a comma because it is a lengthy introductory phrase that precedes the main body of the sentence.)

But:

Last December we wrote to tell you about a new line of guacamole-flavored ice creams we have just developed. (No comma is needed here because the phrase *Last December* is short and refers to place.)

But:

> In 1986, our company had only three employee hot tubs. (The presence of a comma [an option] creates a stronger pause and draws more attention to the year.)

INTERRUPTORS: Changing direction

Guideline. Use a comma to set off short words and phrases that interrupt the flow of the sentence, especially when they contradict, qualify, or amend what has come before.

> We would love to take part in your tango contest. We have just learned, *however*, that we are ineligible to participate. (Commas are needed because *however* interrupts the flow of the sentence.)

> The new plot, *in contrast to the plot we developed last year*, has no loopholes. (Commas are needed here because the phrase *in contrast to the plot we developed last year* interrupts the flow of the sentence.)

A closer look. If you want to deemphasize the pauses that would normally occur as the result of a phrase that interrupts the flow, you can omit the commas.

> We would love to take part in your tango contest. We were planning in fact to hold a contest of our own. (Omitting the commas before and after *in fact* makes the sentence flow more smoothly and quickly but takes the emphasis away from *in fact*.)

COMMAS IN A COMPOUND SENTENCE: Balancing act

Guideline. Use a comma between INDEPENDENT CLAUSES separated by a CONJUNCTION (*and, or, for, but,* etc.) in a COMPOUND SENTENCE. Use your judgment when the clauses are short or the SUBJECT is the same for both clauses.

> Our group has spent the past sixteen months studying the effect that lunar tides have on productivity, and our manager will be delivering her report next Friday. (A comma separates the two clauses because each clause represents an independent thought.)

> I hate the idea, and Dimitri feels the same way. (A comma separates the two clauses because each clause represents an independent thought.)

A closer look. If the two independent clauses in a compound sentence are short and, in particular, if the subject is the same in both, the comma becomes less critical. In general, though, it's a good idea to follow the rule no matter what. This will *prevent* you from writing sentences that read as follows:

> I hate the idea and Dimitri feels the same way.

> I intend to eliminate the problem and Brutus has promised to help.

CLAUSES AND PHRASES IN CONTRAST: Accentuating the negative

Guideline. Use a comma to give more emphasis to a CLAUSE or PHRASE that contradicts or draws a contrast to an earlier idea.

> We introduced the new guacamole-flavored ice cream because we believed in it, *not because we simply wanted to add another flavor to our line*. (Note: If you wanted to give even more emphasis to the clause in italics, you could have used a dash. See page 111.)

COMMAS BEFORE DIRECT QUOTES: Worth quoting

Guideline. Use a comma to separate a direct quote from the word that precedes the quotation.

> Immediately after Brutus spoke at the meeting last night, Cinna stood up and said, "I don't know about you, but I'm out of here." (A comma is needed to separate the quoted statement from the rest of the sentence.)

A closer look. This rule does not apply to indirect quotes. (For more on direct and indirect quotes, see Quotation Marks, page 115.)

> Immediately after Brutus spoke at the meeting last night, Cinna stood up and said that he was leaving. (No comma is needed here because there is no direct quote.)

DIRECT ADDRESS: Personal touch

Guideline. Use a comma to set off the name of anyone you are addressing directly in your writing.

> Let me close this letter, Dimitri, by telling you how pleased we all are with the work you are doing in Bratislava. (Commas are needed to set off *Dimitri*, who is being directly addressed.)

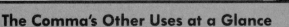

The Comma's Other Uses at a Glance

Situation	Example
Salutation in a friendly letter	Dear Dimitri,
Day from the year	We founded this company on December 14, 1982.
City from a state	Our Midwest headquarters is in Milwaukee, WI.
To separate comparative statements	The more we try to help them, the more they resist.
In place of omitted words	We've called, no answer.
People's names, when reversed	Lincoln, Abraham John, Elton
Numbers in groups of three	Last year's sales totaled more than $2,000,000.
After <u>etc.</u> in the middle of a sentence	We have checked the figures from all the cities, including Chicago, Milwaukee, Atlanta, etc., and we still have been unable to find the problem.

Question Mark

Questionable uses

There are two situations relating to question marks that sometimes create confusion. Here is a look at each.

THE POLITE REQUEST: Asking or telling

Guideline. Sentences that pose a question in the form of a polite request do not necessarily have to end with a question mark. The test is whether the statement demands an answer.

> Would you be kind enough to respond to this invitation as soon as possible. (The question mark is omitted because no answer is required. No one is likely to say, "I will _not_ be kind enough to respond to that invitation.")

INDIRECT QUESTIONS: Telling statements

Guideline. Indirect questions (questions embedded in a straight statement) do not generally end with a question mark.

> Dimitri keeps asking us when he can come home from Bratislava. (A question mark isn't needed here because the sentence is a statement, not a true question.)

But:

> What Dimitri wants to know is, when can he come home from Bratislava? (The question mark is needed because the last element in the sentence is phrased as a question.)

The Colon

Looking ahead

Used properly, the colon lets you do something no other punctuation mark enables you to do as well: produce a pause that alerts the reader to what is about to follow. (The dash can serve this function as well, but the dash does other things, too. It's not as specialized.)

THE COLON BEFORE A LIST: By the numbers

Guideline. Use a colon to create a strong pause between a list of items and the word that introduces the list.

> The order we placed last week included the following items: pencils, pads, paper clips, and a nuclear reactor.

> This fall we plan to visit three cities: Boston, Philadelphia, and Bratislava.

THE COLON AS A SETTING-UP DEVICE: Close encounters

Guideline. Use a colon before a word or an idea that warrants enough emphasis to be set apart from the rest of the sentence.

> The new incentive program offers you something no other program offers: a free trip to Bratislava.

> There is one thing we can't afford to lose: the street map of Bratislava.

THE COLON IN A COMPOUND SENTENCE: Close ties

Guideline. Use a colon in a compound sentence when the second of the two clauses is an amplification or an illustration of the first clause.

> The criticisms you have raised about Brutus are of interest to me: They certainly show how committed you are to our cause. (The idea in the second half of the sentence amplifies the idea presented in the first half.)

> One of the things about the plot that disturbs me is the timetable: There doesn't seem to be enough time to get

from Bratislava to Rome. (The second half of the sentence illustrates the point raised in the first part of the sentence.)

CAPITALIZATION AFTER A COLON: A matter of choice

Guideline. Capitalize the first letter of the first word after a colon only when it is a proper noun or when the group of words itself can stand alone as a sentence. Even then, the choice between a capital and a lowercase letter is optional.

> The plan we are introducing has one feature that no other plan we have ever presented offers: It requires no additional personnel. (*It* has an initial capital because the group of words it introduces could stand alone as a sentence.)

> The plan we are introducing has one feature no other plan we have ever presented offers: very low risk. (No capital letter because *very low risk* is not a complete thought.)

The Apostrophe

Double duty

The apostrophe was originally meant to be used for CONTRACTIONS (*isn't*, *it's*, *they're*, etc.). It still serves that function but it does two other jobs as well. One, it forms the POSSESSIVE of a NOUN; two, it can be used, with *s*, to form the plurals of abbreviations and symbols.

CONTRACTIONS: Missing parts

Guideline. Use an apostrophe in place of the letter or letters that have been removed to form the contraction.

A closer look. The apostrophe does not necessarily go between the two *words* that have been combined. It goes in the space created by removing the letters.

> I *wouldn't* [not *would'nt*] mind the traveling as much if we could rent better camels.

POSSESSIVE NOUNS: Owner's guide

Guideline. Singular nouns form their possessive forms by adding an apostrophe followed by *s*. When the noun is plural, the apostrophe comes after the *s*.

> boy's club (singular)
>
> boys' club (plural)

A closer look. The special considerations to this rule are as follows:

Singular nouns that end in *S*. Forget about the final *s* and treat these nouns the same as other nouns.

> boss's (singular)
>
> bosses' (plural)
>
> Jones's (singular)
>
> Joneses' (plural)

Plural nouns that do not end in *S*. Treat them as if they were singular nouns.

> The *alumni's* response to our invitation has been encouraging.

We're waiting to see the *media's* response to our latest press conference.

COMPOUND OWNERSHIP: Separate tables

Guideline. When both subjects in a compound subject own the same thing, the apostrophe should go with the second subject only. When each owns his or her own thing, an apostrophe must come after each.

> Dimitri and Inga's file is being reviewed. (One file for the two of them.)

> Dimitri's and Inga's files are now being reviewed. (Two files being reviewed.)

The Semicolon

Short stop

The semicolon was more prevalent a century ago when writers were more inclined to write long, intricate, pipe-and-slippers-by-the-fire type sentences. It remains, however, a useful tool in certain situations, and it doesn't hurt to know how and when to use it.

COMPOUND THINKING: Keeping a distance

Guideline. Use a semicolon (sparingly) to separate two independent clauses that are too closely related to warrant a period and not closely related enough to warrant a comma.

> The easy part was coming up with the plot; the hard part was completing it on time.

We never intended the plan to encompass so many details; nor do we think it's a good idea to proceed.

A closer look. Two points are worth stressing about the
semicolon:

First, remember that the clauses a semicolon sepa-
rates must be *independent:* Both clauses should stand on
their own. A semicolon should never be used to separate
a dependent clause from an independent clause, as in:

Despite the rain; [should be a comma] we held the picnic.

Second, the decision to use a semicolon rather than a
comma or period between two independent clauses
shouldn't be influenced by the presence or absence of a
CONJUNCTION—*and, but,* or *or.* Base your decision to use
a semicolon not on the presence or absence of the conjunction, but on how closely you want the two clauses to
relate.

SEMICOLONS IN A SERIES: Keeping a distance

Guideline. Use a semicolon to separate items in a series
when the items are lengthy or complicated.

The speakers who have been signed so far include Louis
George, of Albany, NY; George Albany, of St. George,
NY; and Al York, of Macon, GA.

Dashes and Parentheses

Breaking things up

Dashes and parentheses serve similar functions: They set
apart sentence elements that interrupt the flow of the

sentence. The dash, however, is more versatile. It can be used in many situations that might otherwise call for a comma, a colon, or a semicolon.

The main thing to remember about using either dashes or parentheses is that each disturbs the natural flow of the sentence. Not that this is necessarily a bad thing. It's just that if you go to the well with either device too often, your writing could become disjointed and difficult to follow.

THE DASH IN MID-SENTENCE: Big breaks

Guideline. Use dashes (with restraint) when you want to give added emphasis to a PARENTHETICAL PHRASE or clause.

A closer look. The fact that it is the *widest* of all the punctuation marks explains why the dash does a better job than other marks when it comes to interrupting the flow of the sentence or giving more prominence to the information that either follows it or is enclosed within two dashes.

> The decision to call Dimitri back from Bratislava—and, by the way, I consider it a good decision—was reached two weeks ago.

> All the arrangements concerning next week's coronation—including the order for additional balloons—have already been made.

THE DASH BEFORE A FINAL PHRASE OR CLAUSE: More big breaks

Guideline. Use dashes (again with restraint) to give added emphasis to a phrase or clause that comes at the end of a sentence and serves to contradict or contrast with an earlier idea.

> The decision to call Dimitri back from Bratislava was George's idea—not mine. (The dash creates a stronger break between the two ideas than a comma would have created.)

> Dimitri came because we asked him—not because he wanted to. (Again, the dash gives more emphasis to the contrast.)

DASHES vs. PARENTHESES: Which to use

Guideline. Use dashes when you want to draw attention to the elements and use parentheses when you want to lessen the emphasis.

> Everyone in our company—especially our accountant—thinks we spent much too much money on the Lunar Tides and Productivity Project. (Dashes draw more attention to the accountant's opinion.)

> Everyone in our company (especially our accountant) thinks we spent much too much money on the Lunar Tides and Productivity Project. (Parentheses make the mention of the accountant seem more a whisper than a shout.)

> All our offices—even the normally quiet office in Vesuvius—have been busy this month. (more emphasis)

> All of our offices (even the normally quiet office in Vesuvius) have been busy this month. (less emphasis)

The Hyphen

Dividing lines

The primary job of the hyphen is to connect compound words, which makes it as much a spelling tool as a punctuation tool. Its other use, of course, is to separate the syllables of words that start on one line and finish on the next.

COMPOUND WORDS: Close encounters

Guideline. When compound ADJECTIVES (two adjectives that act as a single modifier) precede a NOUN, separate them with hyphens. When they follow the VERB and stand on their own, leave the hyphens out.

> My friend Iago is a *quick-thinking, hard-to-please* young man [hyphenated because the adjectives act as single modifiers and precede the noun *man*] who, at the same time, is soft spoken and mild mannered [no hyphens because the modifiers follow the verb, *is*, and stand on their own].

A closer look. Many common compound adjectives are always hyphenated, regardless of how—and where—they are used. These include:

> left-hand (and right-hand)
> left-handed (and right-handed)
> twenty-one (and all other numbers up to ninety-nine)
> two-thirds (and other fractions)
> self-righteous (and most other words that begin with the prefix *self-*)

Quotation Marks

On the record

The main function of quotation marks is to let your readers know that the information you are presenting originated from someone or something other than you, whether it be a person, a magazine article, or a book. Quotation marks have other uses having to do with titles of certain types of work, but their application in these situations varies according to which style book you choose to follow. Here are the key points to keep in mind.

INDIRECT QUOTES: Not quite the same

Guideline. Use quotation marks for statements that are being quoted verbatim and not when you are simply paraphrasing what someone said.

> When I spoke to Dimitri last week, he said, "I hate Bratislava." (Quote marks because Dimitri is being quoted verbatim.)

> When I spoke to Dimitri last week, he told me that he didn't like Bratislava. (No quotes: Dimitri's comments are being paraphrased.)

But:

> When I spoke to Dimitri last week, he told me that he "hated" Bratislava. (Quotes acceptable since Dimitri presumably used the word "hate.")

Quotation Marks: How the Other Marks Fit In

Mark	Guideline	Examples
Period	Always inside	Inga was optimistic. She said, "It looks good."
Comma	Always inside	"It looks good," she said.
Question mark	Inside when the question mark applies to the quote only	Nero then asked, "Can you do it?"
	Outside when the question mark applies to the whole sentence	Weren't you the one who asked, "Can we do it"?
Exclamation point	Inside if it applies to the quoted material	Brutus then stood up and said, "I quit!"
	Outside if it applies to the whole sentence	I won't stand for people who say "I quit"!
Semicolon	Usually outside, unless it is part of the quoted material	I read the article "Running Successful Tango Contests"; it was quite revealing.

Quotation Marks: How the Other Marks Fit In (con't.)

Mark	Guideline	Examples
Colon	Usually outside, unless it is part of the quoted material	The following points should be discussed about the article "Customer Service": one, the importance of keeping in touch, etc.
Dash	Usually outside	The article she quoted—"Ice Cream Flavor Trends for the 1990s"—made several interesting points.
Parentheses	Outside, except when the parenthetical element is part of the quotation	He quoted the famous FDR statement ("The only thing we have to fear is fear itself") before leaving. The article "Trends for the 1990s (Part I)" makes several interesting points.

Punctuation at a Glance

Mark	Main Uses	Examples
Apostrophe	■ Contractions	We can't attend.
	■ To show possession in nouns	Inga's new boss
Colon	■ To signal a pause that introduces a series	The model comes in three colors: gray, red, and brown.
	■ To stress a word, phrase, or clause that follows	We want to do this for a simple reason: The company needs it.
Comma	■ To separate items in a series	We are looking for new computers, new printers, and new software.
	■ To separate nonessential phrases and clauses from the rest of the sentence	At your request, we are sending you the latest revisions.
	■ To set off a phrase or clause that contrasts with or contradicts what has come before	We are not going to bid on the job, not unless things change.
	■ To separate two independent clauses in a compound sentence	The situation is improving, but we still need to remain alert.

Punctuation at a Glance (con't.)

Mark	Main Uses	Examples
Dash	■ To indicate a sharp break in a thought	If everything goes right—and we think it will—we will be done today.
Exclamation point	■ To mark the end of a sentence that expresses an exclamation	This is terrible!
Hyphen	■ To combine words (mostly two or more adjectives preceding a noun)	out-of-date mini-review
Parentheses	■ To enclose within a sentence information that is incidental to the main thought but is still worth expressing	The procedure doesn't take long (an hour or two at the most).
Period	■ To mark the end of a sentence that is neither a question nor an exclamation	The shipment has arrived. Make sure you send it as soon as possible.

(con't.)

Punctuation at a Glance (con't.)

Mark	Main Uses	Examples
Question mark	■ To mark the end of a question	When may we expect your call?
Quotation marks	■ To indicate the start and end of quoted material	Liza said, "I'm not going."
	■ To enclose titles of articles, essays, etc., appearing in larger works	"The End of an Era" is the most interesting chapter in the book.
Semicolon	■ To separate independent clauses not joined by *and* or *but*	Most of the employees are in favor of the plan; still, management has its doubts.
	■ To separate items in a series that are themselves separated by commas	The speakers included George Adams, from Kentucky; Louise Phillips, from Georgia; and Lisa George, from New York.

QUOTING FOR EFFECT: Not a "good" idea

Guideline. Avoid the practice of putting words in quotes merely to draw attention to the idea the word is meant to convey. Be especially careful about using quote marks to tell your reader that you are using a particular word in order to be humorous or sarcastic (as I have done in the heading).

What *not* to do:

> All of us on the sixth floor have been "pulling together" this week because we are all "concerned" about Dimitri, and we don't like the "idea" that he is still in Bratislava, which is clearly not his "favorite" city.

Exclamation Points

Nailing down

The exclamation point has one function only: to give added punch to a sentence that makes a particularly strong point. The main thing to bear in mind about using it is to use it sparingly!

CHAPTER 6

Spellbound

How to be letter perfect (well, almost) when you write

Hardly anybody has anything nice to say about the way spelling works in English. But what else can you expect from a language in which there are roughly 40 different phonetic sounds that can be produced by more than 200 different letter combinations? George Bernard Shaw drove home this point as convincingly as anyone when he showed how the word *fish* could logically be spelled *ghoti:* with the initial *f* taking its sound from the *gh* in *tough;* the *i* sounding like the *o* in *women;* and the *sh* sounding like the *ti* in *negotiate*.

So much for the depressing news. The good news, apart from the fact that the spell-checking programs in word processors keep getting smarter, is that there is more logic to English spelling than most people think.

First of all, there is a handful of spelling rules that actually work—if you take the time to learn them and use them. Second, the number of words that defy conventional phonetic principles narrows considerably when you eliminate from consideration two categories of words: highly technical terms and those tongue-twister words that surface only in spelling bees and Scrabble tournaments.

Consider this: If you were to decide today that you were going to spend ten minutes a day studying a handful of the most commonly misspelled words in English, in less than a month you would move up to the top rung of American spellers. This chapter will help you get started.

(Note: For spelling, our authority is *Webster's Ninth New Collegiate Dictionary,* which is based on the unabridged *Webster's Third New International Dictionary.*)

Rules Worth Remembering

A handful of spelling rules that—guess what!—really work

I BEFORE *E*: Old standby

Guideline. This familiar rule—*i* before *e*, except after *c*—works most of the time:

I before *e*	Except after *c*
believe	conceive
grieve	deceive
relief	perceive
siege	receive
thief	
yield	

The exceptions to this rule are words in which the *ei* is pronounced the same as a long *a* or a long *i:*

> height (pronounced like a long *i*)
> neighbor (pronounced like a long *a*)
> surveillance (pronounced like a long *a*)
> weight (pronounced like a long *a*)

PREFIXES: Standing pat

Guideline. Adding a PREFIX rarely affects the spelling of the root word.

A closer look. This is one of those rare spelling rules in English for which there are almost no exceptions. Keep it in mind and it will prevent you from misspelling dozens of commonly misspelled words (including *misspelled*) in which the final letter of the prefix is also the first letter of the root word. Here's a list of some of those words:

Prefix	Root Word	Word
dis	satisfied	dissatisfied
dis	similar	dissimilar
il	legal	illegal
il	legible	illegible
il	literate	illiterate
il	logical	illogical
im	mobile	immobile
im	modest	immodest
im	moral	immoral
ir	relevant	irrelevant
ir	reparable	irreparable
mis	shapen	misshapen
non	negotiable	nonnegotiable
over	reach	overreach
over	run	overrun
un	natural	unnatural
un	necessary	unnecessary
un	nerve	unnerve

SUFFIXES AND WORDS ENDING IN *E:* Easing up

Guideline. When adding a SUFFIX to a word that ends in *e*, keep the final *e* if the first letter of the suffix is a consonant. Drop the *e* if the first letter of the suffix is a vowel.

A closer look. This normally reliable rule does not apply to words in which the final *e* is preceded by one of the following four letters: *c*, *e*, *g*, *o*, and the first letter of the suffix is a vowel.

■ Words whose suffixes begin with consonants (the final *e* stays):

Root	Suffix	Word
achieve	ment	achievement
nine	ty	ninety
rule	bound	rulebound
sincere	ly	sincerely
type	set	typeset

■ Words whose suffixes begin with vowels (the final *e* is dropped):

Root	Suffix	Word
achieve	able	achievable
dispense	able	dispensable
rule	er	ruler
type	ist	typist

Exceptions: words in which the final *e* is preceded by *c*, *e*, *g*, or *o* (the final *e* stays):

Root	Suffix	Word
agree	ing	agreeing
change	able	changeable
manage	able	manageable
outrage	ous	outrageous
notice	able	noticeable
toe	ing	toeing

SUFFIXES AND THE FINAL CONSONANT: Double trouble

Guideline. Double the final consonant of a two-syllable word when the accent falls on the final syllable and the suffix begins with a vowel. Otherwise don't double it.

A closer look. This rule applies mainly to two-syllable words in which the final consonant is preceded by a vowel.

Root	Suffix	Word
ad*mit*	ance	admittance
con*trol*	ing	controlling
oc*cur*	ed	occurred
oc*cur*	ence	occurrence
o*mit*	ing	omitting
re*fer*	al	referral
re*pel*	ent	repellent

■ Words in which the accent falls on the first syllable (the consonant isn't doubled):

Root	Suffix	Word
*cre*dit	or	creditor
*or*der	ing	ordering
*pro*fit	ed	profited

Exceptions: words in which the final consonant is doubled, even though the accent is on the first syllable:

Root	Suffix	Word
*kid*nap	ing	kidnapping
*side*step	ing	sidestepping

SHORT WORDS AND SUFFIXES: Double time

Guideline. Double the final consonant of single-syllable words in which the consonant is preceded by a vowel.

Root	Suffix	Word
bid	er	bidder
hit	er	hitter
run	ing	running

WHEN WORDS END IN *C:* Playing hardball

Guideline. When a word ends in hard *c* (pronounced *keh*) and is preceded by a vowel, add a *k* to maintain the hard sound.

Root	Suffix	Word
colic	y	colic*k*y
panic	ing	panic*k*ing
picnic	er	picnic*k*er
traffic	ed	traffic*k*ed

Group Therapy

How to spell plurals that don't follow the standard rule (which says to add an s to the root)

SPECIAL ENDINGS: Added touches

Guideline. Words ending in *ch*, *x*, or *s* form their plurals by adding *es*, forming another syllable.

Singular	Plural
boss	bosses
catch	catches
pass	passes
tax	taxes

WORDS THAT END IN *Y:* Catching flies

Guideline. Words ending in *y* (when the *y* is preceded by a consonant) change the *y* to *ie* before adding *s*.

Singular	Plural
city	cities
cry	cries
fly	flies
lady	ladies
reply	replies

COMPOUNDS LINKED TO MODIFIERS: First choice

Guideline. Most compound words form their plurals by adding the *s* to the most important word in the compound—usually the first word.

Singular	Plural
justice-of-the-peace	justices-of-the-peace
writer-in-residence	writers-in-residence
son-in-law	sons-in-law

LATIN OR GREEK ENDINGS: When in Rome

Guideline. Most words of Greek and Latin origin that end in *um* or *on* form their plurals by dropping the *um* or *on* and adding *a*. There are, however, a few of these words that form their plurals by adding *s* to the singular form. What you *don't* want to do is to add both an *a* and an *s*. That would form, in effect, a double plural.

Singular	Plural
addendum	addend*a*
criterion	criteri*a* (not criteri*as*)
curriculum	curricul*a*
datum (rare)	dat*a* (always plural)
erratum	errat*a*
medium (used in connection with communication)	medi*a*
medium (used in connection with those who communicate with the dead)	medium*s*
memorandum	memorand*a* or memorandum*s* (but not memorand*as*)
phenomenon	phenomen*a* (never phenomen*as*)
ultimatum	ultimat*ums*

INITIALS: Keeping it simple

Guideline. Numbers, letters, and abbreviations usually form their plurals by adding lowercase *s*.

Singular	Plural
MBA	MBAs
MD	MDs
RN	RNs

Spelling Demons

In a class by themselves

(Note: The following spelling demons have been grouped according to the letters or groups of letters that make them difficult to spell. For a complete list of the toughest words to spell in English, see page 134–35.)

■ **Doubling up.** Words in which certain letters are (or aren't) repeated.

accidenta*ll*y	o*pp*ortunity
a*cc*o*mm*odate	para*ll*el
ba*tt*a*l*ion	questio*nn*aire
*comm*i*tt*ee	reco*mm*end
emba*rr*a*ss*ed	sate*ll*ite
ha*r*a*ss*ed	syste*m*atic
mi*ll*e*nn*ium	wri*tt*en

■ **Ible & Able.** Words ending in the suffixes -*able* and -*ible*. (*Able* is the more common of the two, but you can't always play the odds.)

Able	Ible
comparable	compatible
dependable	credible
likable	flexible
probable	irresistible
reliable	possible
	sensible

■ *E, I, & A: Soundalikes.* Words in which *a*, *e*, and *i* are all pronounced the same.

A	E	I
acquaintance	absence	definite
advantage	coincidence	infinite
attendance	confident	
balance	existence	
calendar	occurrence	
maintenance	prevalent	
relevant		

■ **Phantoms.** Words that include a letter which isn't pronounced (the phantom letter or letters is in italics).

ai*s*le	j*e*opardy
ans*w*er	l*ie*utenant
co*l*onel	lunch*e*on
de*b*t	mor*t*gage
ga*u*ge	r*h*ythm
g*u*ard	su*b*tlety
hemorr*h*age	

■ **Foreign-born.** Words that have been imported from other languages, such as:

aficionado	khaki
chutzpah	liaison
connoisseur	reconnaissance
entrepreneur	reconnoiter
financier	renaissance

Spelling Demons: The Most Commonly Misspelled Words in English

absence	bankruptcy	coolly	environment	graffiti
accidentally	believe	council (group)	escrow	grammar
accommodate	boulevard	counsel (advisor, lawyer)	excellent	grievance
accumulate	boundary		exercise	gruesome
achievement	buses	courageous	existence	guarantee
acknowledgment	business	criticism	exonerate	
acquaintance			extension	harass
acquiesce	calendar	deceive	eyeing	height
affect	capital	deductible		hors d'oeuvre
aggravate	capitol (building)	definite	facsimile	
all right	carriage	descendant	February	ignorant
amateur	cemetery	desert (place)	fiery	impasse
analogous	census	dessert (food)	financier	indispensable
analysis	coincidence	dining	fluorescent	innocuous
appall	commitment	disappointed	foresee	inoculate
apparatus	committee	dissatisfied	foreword	irrelevant
appreciable	concede		forfeit	itinerary
architecture	condominium	effect	forth	
argument	connoisseur	eighth	forty	judgment
athletic	conscientious	eligible	fourth	
attendance	conscious	embarrassed		knowledge
auxiliary	consensus	entrepreneur	gauge	
		enumerate	government	laboratory

Spelling Demons: (con't.)

leisure	occasion	pronunciation	schedule	surveillance
liable	occurred	publicly	scissors	susceptible
liaison	occurrence		secede	tariff
library	omitted	questionnaire	seize	temperamental
license	optimistic	quiet	separate	theater
lien	original	quite	siege	threshold
lieutenant			similar	tragedy
liquefy	parallel	rarefy	solely	truly
literature	pastime	receive	souvenir	
loose	penitentiary	recommend	sponsor	unmanageable
lose	perhaps	referred	stationary	unwieldy
losing	perseverance	relevant	(standing still)	usage
	persistent	relieve	stationery	
maintenance	phenomenal	reminiscence	(writer's paper)	vacillate
marriage	phenomenon	renaissance	strength	
memento	prairie	renowned	subtlety	Wednesday
minuscule	preceding	rescind	subtly	weird
mischievous	prerogative	restaurateur	succeed	whether
misspell	principal	rhythm	suing	wholly
	principle		superintendent	wield
necessary	privilege	sacrilegious	supersede	woman
neutral	proceed	satellite	surreptitious	
noticeable				yield

CHAPTER 7

Changing Times

*Six grammar rules you can
safely bend*

Most people agree that if a language is to work, it
needs a structure—a body of rules that users are familiar
with and are willing to follow with reasonable consis-
tency. But what do you do about a rule that has worked
its way into the system but is no longer in step with the
way the language is actually used? And what do you do
about rules or principles that, in retrospect, should never
have come into being in the first place?

In this chapter, we'll take a look at six rules that fall into one of these two categories. You have probably heard of most of these rules, and a few of them may still be part of the instructional baggage you carry with you when you speak or write.

Keep in mind that each of these principles has some validity. It isn't the rule itself that's the problem, in other words; it's the knots you can tie yourself into if you follow the rule too blindly. I am not advocating that you disregard the principles that follow—only that you view them as guidelines and not rules to live—and die—by.

1. Never End a Sentence with a Preposition

The notion that ending a sentence with a preposition is grammatical heresy was originally advanced more than three centuries ago by the venerated English poet and essayist John Dryden. Dryden, a Latin scholar, based his view on the fact that prepositions are never found at the end of sentences written in Latin. And given Dryden's reputation, it is no surprise that his sentiments forged their way into the grammar texts of the eighteenth and nineteenth centuries and eventually into the grammar classrooms of the twentieth century.

But here's the problem. Neither Dryden nor the grammarians who promoted his views envisioned the extent to which many of the most commonly used prepositions—*on, to, in, about, over, of,* etc.—would hook up with verbs to become common idioms. Nor did they take into account the awkwardness that results when you run one of these verb-preposition idioms through the never-end-a-sentence-with-a-preposition wringer.

Examples:

Ophelia is someone everybody looks up to.
Ophelia is someone up to whom everybody looks.

What are you talking about?
About what are you talking?

Or the often-quoted Winston Churchill retort:

This is the sort of impertinence up with which I will not put.

Yes, there are good reasons for keeping prepositions away from the end of a sentence, especially when the preposition is redundant, as in:

Where are you working _at_?

Where will you be _at_?

Generally, though, your ear will tell you when to follow John Dryden's advice and, more important, when it is advice to which you do not have to pay attention or about which you do not have to worry (just kidding!).

2. Never Split an Infinitive

You split an infinitive by inserting a modifier—an adverb, usually—between the _to_ and the _verb_, as in "I want you _to_ carefully _read_ over these instructions." The notion that this incision is grammatically unsound was first set forth in the mid-1800s, and it, too, finds its basis in Latin, a language in which the infinitive is a one-word verb form.

Keeping infinitives intact is actually a sensible idea.

Otherwise you run the risk of writing sentences that sound like this:

> We wanted to, because we felt it was important, talk to you today about our Lunar Tides and Productivity Project.

Still, no grammarian today sees any value in having an *official* sanction against splitting infinitives, and everyone agrees that it was a silly rule to adopt in the first place. Even if the rule didn't exist, split infinitives would rarely occur; that's because we rarely split them in conversation. On the other hand, there are certain situations in which splitting the infinitive produces precisely the effect you want to produce, which is to put less emphasis on the action conveyed in the infinitive and more on the modifier.

Examples:

> I would now like you to slowly and precisely tell me what happened and how it happened. (Splitting the infinitive positions the adverbs *slowly* and *precisely* immediately before the verb *tell* and puts the emphasis on these two words.)

3. Never Use Two Negatives in the Same Sentence

The logic behind this rule is that two negatives in the same construction cancel each other out. When we say, "We never did nothing," what we are saying, in effect, is that "At no time did we ever do nothing," which means that at all times we did something. Something like that, anyway.

The problem with this otherwise logical rule is that it fails to make a crucial distinction: the difference between double negatives that occur in the same clause, and double negatives that occur in a sentence that has two clauses, each with its own negative expression.

Here's an example:

> It is *not* that we do *not* favor your plan to open a new branch office in Bratislava. It is just that we think your plan has too many complications. (This is acceptable English because the two negatives in the first sentence are part of different clauses.)

> We *never* intended *not* to share with you the results of our study. (Again, the two negatives are part of different clauses.)

But:

> We *never* wanted *no* trouble from you. (Not acceptable English because both negatives are part of the same clause.)

4. Don't Repeat Words; Use Synonyms Instead

Going out of your way to avoid using a word you have already used a few words earlier was useful advice when you were writing school papers and one of your agendas was to impress your English teachers with the size and range of your vocabulary. It is also a good principle to follow when it comes to certain types of words and expressions—phrases such as "on the other hand," "to make a long story short," "of course"—and, in particular, "like" and "you know."

In general, though, going out of your way to *avoid* repeating words—this practice is sometimes referred to as "elegant variation"—is counterproductive. Repeating a key word several times in a paragraph is often the glue that gives a well-written paragraph its cohesion. And repetition can work effectively as a rhetorical device. It can produce a nicely balanced flow to your sentences and can give added impact to key points. Consider whether the following examples would have had the same impact if the speakers had followed the advice contained in this rule.

We have nothing to fear but alarm itself.

You can fool all the people some of the time and a few individuals in every instance; but it is impossible to trick each human being in the absolutely largest number of situations.

We shall not flag or fail. We shall fight in France, we shall battle on the seas and oceans, we shall contend with growing confidence and growing strength in the air, we shall defend our island, whatever the cost may be, we shall contest on the beaches, we shall struggle on the landing grounds, we shall make combat in the fields and in the streets, we shall duel in the hills; we shall never surrender.

The defense rests.

5. Avoid the Use of "I" in Business Correspondence

There are three reasons why many people find it difficult to use the first-person pronoun in anything other than a love letter.

Reason number one is the ill-conceived and clearly out-of-date notion that business correspondence is too dignified a means of communication to warrant the use of a word as common and plebeian as "I."

Reason number two is the equally ill-conceived notion that if you use "I" in a memo or letter, people will think you are stuck on yourself.

Reason number three is that it is grammatically "wrong" to use the word "I" in anything other than a personal letter or a first-person essay.

These are all myths. The probable explanation behind them is that many elementary and high school English teachers, in an effort to get their pupils to differentiate an opinion from a fact, often forbid their students to use *I*.

Whatever the reason, this is one principle whose validity is limited to only a handful of situations, chief among them technical and financial reports, and formal proposals. Going out of your way to avoid "I" in any correspondence in which you have been *asked* to offer opinions is silly.

Avoiding "I" in sales correspondence is worse than silly, it is bad business. In most sales writing, your main objective is to establish a strong personal connection between you and your reader. *I* and *you* are better suited for that job than any other two words in the English language.

6. Never Start a Sentence with *And* or *But*

Nobody seems to know how or where this widely espoused principle of "good writing" ever got off the ground. The best explanation is that it takes root when teachers try to disabuse grade-schoolers from stringing together *every* sentence they write with one *and* after another.

Here, again, we have a guideline worth keeping in mind but self-defeating if you follow it to the letter.

Starting an occasional sentence with *and* is an easy and effective way to smooth out the transition from one sentence to the next. If there were anything grammatically unhealthy about the practice, the Bible would be forbidden reading in most grammar schools.

As for *but*, it is a simple and forceful way to start any sentence whose information contradicts or qualifies the information conveyed in the previous sentence— much better, by the way, than *however*. That's why it is used so often in newspaper and magazine articles.

Should you go out of your way to start sentences with *and* or *but?* No. Using either of these words to open a sentence is simply a device, and like any device, it will lose its impact and is likely to become a distraction if you use it too often. But *never* using either of these words at the beginning of a sentence doesn't serve either *your* best interests or the best interests of your readers.

CHAPTER 8

Finishing Touches

How not to sweat the details

Many of the usage decisions that need to be made in day-to-day correspondence have less to do with grammar and more to do with convention and style—and, in particular, with how a company or organization likes to see things done. Some organizations publish their own style-books, and there are a half-dozen or so books on the market that describe in excruciating detail how a particular newspaper or publisher ought to treat such issues as abbreviations, capitalization, numbers, and so forth.

This final chapter looks at some of the questions that arise most often in these various usage categories. Keep in mind that what we say here may not be consistent with how your company chooses to handle a specific situation. Keep in mind, too, that the guidelines we offer are simply a reflection of how most style manuals view a specific issue. They are not meant to be the final word on what is appropriate or inappropriate.

Abbreviations

Abbreviation-related issues that often produce confusion

(Note: A list of the most commonly used abbreviations appears on page 147–151.)

MAKING THE CHOICE: When to abbreviate (and when not to)

Guideline. Abbreviate only those words that have legitimate abbreviations, and keep in mind that even when they are legitimate, too many abbreviations in a sentence will make it difficult to read.

> The oasis is only *two miles* [not *2 mi.*] away and we should be there in less than *an hour* [not *an hr.*].

A closer look. The shorter the word, the more you should think twice before abbreviating it. The exception: when you're using short words—generally units of measurement—over and over in a list or in tabular material.

ABBREVIATIONS AND PERIODS: Capital gains

Guideline. Use periods after abbreviations in which all the letters are lowercase, but not after abbreviations in which all the letters are uppercase.

> When the _FBI_ heard that we were sending the reactor _c.o.d.,_ they naturally contacted the _UN_. But because it was 2 _p.m_. I was talking at the time to the AT&T representative and I didn't pay attention.

A closer look. Be alert to the handful of lowercase abbreviations that _never_ have periods:

> rpm
> mph
> cc

ABBREVIATIONS AT THE END OF A SENTENCE: How many periods?

Guideline. When an abbreviation followed by a period comes at the end of a sentence that would normally end with a period, the sentence-ending period is usually _dropped_. If the statement is a question or an exclamation, it should end with the appropriate mark.

> I would like you to send me the nuclear reactor c.o.d.

But:

> Would you like us to send it to you c.o.d.?

> I can't believe that Dimitri sent the reactor c.o.d.!

Common Abbreviations

Note: Whether you use periods with many abbreviations has become increasingly a matter of company style or personal preference. The newer dictionaries tend to omit most periods, except when the omission would create an abbreviation that looks like another word.

Business terms

as soon as possible	ASAP
carbon copy (to)	cc
cash on delivery	c.o.d.
Company	Co.
credit	cr.
department	dept.
district	dis.
doing business as	DBA
each	ea.
fiscal year	FY
for example	e.g.
for your information	FYI
Incorporated	Inc.
manufacturing	mfg.
merchandise	mdse.
postscript	PS
quarter	qtr.
that is	i.e.

Compass points

East	E
North	N
South	S
West	W

Days of the week

Monday	Mon.
Tuesday	Tue.
Wednesday	Wed.
Thursday	Thur.
Friday	Fri.
Saturday	Sat.
Sunday	Sun.

Months

January	Jan.
February	Feb.
March	Mar.
April	Apr.
May	May
June	June
July	July
August	Aug.
September	Sept.
October	Oct.
November	Nov.
December	Dec.

Titles, degrees, etc.

Assistant	Asst.
Bachelor of Arts	B.A.
Bachelor of Science	B.S.
Captain	Capt.
Colonel	Col.
Democrat	Dem.
Doctor	Dr.
Doctor of Dental Surgery	DDS
Doctor of Divinity	D.D.
Doctor of Education	Ed.D.
Doctor of Law	LL.D. or J.D.

Doctor of Medicine	M.D.
Doctor of Philosophy	Ph.D.
Esquire	Esq.
General	Gen.
Governor	Gov.
Honorable	Hon.
Lieutenant	Lt.
manager	mgr.
Master of Arts	M.A.
Master of Science	M.S.
Mechanical Engineer	M.E.
Private	Pvt.
Registered Nurse	R.N.
Reverend	Rev.
Saint	St.
Saint (feminine)	Ste.
secretary	sec.
Senior	Sr.
Sergeant	Sgt.
Treasurer	Treas.
Vice President	V.P.

U.S. States and Territories

Note: States can be abbreviated in one of two ways. The more recently developed two-letter abbreviations were originally meant to be used for addresses only, but they are gradually becoming acceptable in general correspondence as well. We've listed both. When an abbreviation in parentheses has been omitted, it means that no abbreviation exists.

Alabama (Ala.)	AL
Alaska (Alas.)	AK
Arizona (Ariz.)	AZ
Arkansas (Ark.)	AR
California (Cal.)	CA
Canal Zone	CZ

Colorado (Colo.)	CO
Connecticut (Conn.)	CT
Delaware (Del.)	DE
District of Columbia	DC
Florida (Fla.)	FL
Georgia (Ga.)	GA
Guam	GU
Hawaii (Haw.)	HI
Idaho (Ida.)	ID
Illinois (Ill.)	IL
Indiana (Ind.)	IN
Iowa (Io.)	IA
Kansas (Kans.)	KS
Kentucky (Ky.)	KY
Louisiana (La.)	LA
Maine (Me.)	ME
Maryland (Md.)	MD
Massachusetts (Mass.)	MA
Michigan (Mich.)	MI
Minnesota (Minn.)	MN
Mississippi (Miss.)	MS
Missouri (Mo.)	MO
Montana (Mont.)	MT
Nebraska (Nebr.)	NE
Nevada (Nev.)	NV
New Hampshire (N.H.)	NH
New Jersey (N.J.)	NJ
New Mexico (N.M.)	NM
New York (N.Y.)	NY
North Carolina (N.C.)	NC
North Dakota (N.D.)	ND
Ohio	OH
Oklahoma (Okla.)	OK
Oregon (Oreg.)	OR

Pennsylvania (Penn.)	PA
Puerto Rico (P.R.)	PR
Rhode Island (R.I.)	RI
South Carolina (S.C.)	SC
South Dakota (S. Dak.)	SD
Tennessee (Tenn.)	TN
Texas (Tex.)	TX
Utah	UT
Vermont (Vt.)	VT
Virgin Islands (V.I.)	VI
Virginia (Va.)	VA
Washington (Wash.)	WA
West Virginia (W. Va.)	WV
Wisconsin (Wis.)	WI
Wyoming (Wyo.)	WY

Capitalization

Standing tall

The main reason for starting any word with a capital letter is to accord it more importance than words that begin with lowercase letters. The principles that govern which words ought to be capitalized—and when—are reasonably fixed and fairly well known, but there are dozens of instances in which the decision is a matter of preference or of company style. Here are some of those situations.

JOB TITLES: Climbing the ladder

Guideline. Barring company rules to the contrary, use lowercase letters for job titles when the titles merely describe a job. Capitalize them when they precede a person's name or are part of a phrase used to identify the person.

> The recent conference on lunar tides and productivity drew more than 200 directors of human resources [not Directors of Human Resources].

> Inga Adams, Director of Human Resources, was one of the attendees. (Capitalized because it identifies the person as having a specific title.)

> Most of the senior analysts [not Senior Analysts] in the company were excited by the results of the study.

A closer look. Unless your job depends on it, resist the temptation to base job title capitalization decisions on the importance of the position. This means that if you don't intend to capitalize "mail room supervisor," think twice about capitalizing "vice president of marketing." This guideline should also apply to the president of the company. As a general rule, "president" should begin with a capital letter only when it refers to the specific person occupying the White House (speaking of other terms that should be capitalized in certain situations only).

> Our company president is on a first-name basis with the President (assuming it's the President of the United States).

> There were several corporate presidents at the baths last night.

WORDS THAT SWING BOTH WAYS: Common sense

Guideline. Be alert to words that should be capitalized in some situations, but not in others. Consult a dictionary to verify the proper form.

> Father Leo, a _Catholic_ priest, is a man with _catholic_ tastes.

> What surprised me about _France_ was how hard it is to find shirts with _french cuffs_.

> Just about everyone I met during my visit to _Oxford_ was wearing an _oxford_ gray suit.

RACES AND ETHNIC GROUPS: Mix and match

Guideline. Capitalize racial groups when referring to a specific race (Caucasian, Negroid, etc.), but not when racial terms are used in a more general sense.

A closer look. There are sharp differences of opinion over whether the _b_ in _black,_ when _black_ is used to identify a racial group, ought to be capitalized. The argument in favor of capitalization is that _black_ is now used in situations that would have previously called for _Negro._ The argument against capitalizing _black_ is that you would then have to capitalize _white_ when used in the same context. Stay tuned.

DIRECTIONS: Low profile

Guideline. Don't capitalize east, west, north, and south—unless the term is part of the name of an actual city or country, or refers to a specific region of the world that incorporates a group of countries.

> We used to have an office in _East St. Louis_ but we decided to move a little farther _west_ so that we could take advantage of the growing market in the _southern_ part of _South Dakota_.

> We plan to introduce our new ice cream flavors in the _Far East_ next year.

REFERENCES TO TIME: Season's greetings

Guideline. Always capitalize the days of the week and the months of the year, but use lowercase letters when referring to winter, spring, summer, and fall.

> On _Monday, January_ 14, we will be holding our annual _mid-winter_ flamenco shoes auction, and we know that it will be every bit as exciting as our _spring_ auction, which we ran last _May_.

Numbers' Game

Either or

There are two ways to express numbers in writing: One is to spell them out; the other is to express them in Arabic numerals.

BASIC CHOICES: Is it "2" or "two"?

Guideline. The generally followed guideline (and there are exceptions galore) is to write the number out when the number you are expressing is between _one_ and _nine_, and to use Arabic numbers for numbers above _nine_.

> I counted _eight_ [less than 10] horses and _23_ [more than 10] of the king's men.

A closer look. Here are some specific situations and the guidelines to apply in each.

■ **Large numbers.** Use cardinal (spelled out) numbers for very large (in the millions) rounded-off numbers. Use Arabic numbers when the number gets complicated.

> There are roughly *ten million* [large, rounded-off number] tango dancers in the world, but only *552* [more complicated] live in Bratislava.

■ **Money.** Use mostly Arabic numbers, except when you are expressing large, rounded-off numbers or talking about money in general terms.

> We have spent more than *$2 million* [rounded-off number] on the Lunar Tides and Productivity Project, compared to *$750,000* [more complicated] last year and *several million dollars* [general terms] the year before.

■ **Dates and time.** Use Arabic numbers for most times and dates. Exceptions: in formal correspondence (invitations, for example), or when the number is the first word in the sentence.

> The flamenco dancers upstairs have been practicing steps that date back to *1722*, but I wish they wouldn't practice these steps at *2:30* a.m.

> *Two-thirty* [first word in sentence] in the morning [not 2:30 a.m.] is not a good time to practice flamenco dancing.

Appendix

One of the best books ever written about English grammar—George Curme's *A Grammar of the English Language*—consists of two volumes and runs more than 1,000 pages, with nearly 100 pages devoted to verbs alone.

The scope of this section is rather more limited. It is to Curme's work what a CPR course is to medical school. The first part is a crash course in the really *basic* basics of grammar—the concepts that crop up time and again in usage situations. The second section is a glossary of the grammar terms used throughout this book.

Basic Training

The eight core concepts of English grammar:

1. The sentence
2. The subject and predicate
3. The complement
4. Clauses and phrases
5. The parts of speech
6. The difference between action and linking verbs
7. The difference between verbs and verbals
8. The difference between adjectives and adverbs

1. THE SENTENCE: Thoughts apart

Definition. The sentence is best defined as a group of words that can stand on its own as a completed thought, reasonably separate from the words that precede it or that come after it. That's the *classic* definition. The problem with this definition is that in many forms of writing— fiction or advertising copy, for instance—writers take liberties with the definition and often write sentences that contain a single word.

Generally, though, if you stick to the standard definition, you will avoid the common problem of expressing ideas in fragments instead of sentences. Notice the differences in the following:

> Every cloud has a silver lining. (This qualifies as a sentence because it expresses a complete thought.)

> When the clouds roll by. (This is a fragment: It expresses only a partial thought.)

Life is just a bowl of cherries. (This qualifies as a sentence because it expresses a complete thought.)

A bowl of cherries. (This is a fragment: It expresses only a partial thought.)

A closer look. Sentences generally have the following characteristics:

■ They begin with a capital letter and end with a PERIOD, a QUESTION MARK, or an EXCLAMATION POINT.

■ They always include at least one SUBJECT and its VERB (see below), although in some cases one or the other of these elements can be omitted—as long as its presence is understood.

Don't go away mad. (The subject of this sentence [you] is understood.)

■ They can express a simple statement, a command, or a question.

Life is a bowl of cherries. (statement)

Give me those cherries. (command)

Do you like cherries? (question)

2. THE SUBJECT & PREDICATE: Building blocks

Definition. The SUBJECT and PREDICATE are the building blocks of every thought. The subject is the word or words that represent what the thought is about. The predicate is the word or words that represent what is being said about the subject.

A closer look. Some general observations about subjects and predicates:

■ The term *subject* can apply to either the key word in the subject *(simple subject)* or the key word along with all the other words that relate to it *(complete subject)*. It is always something you can name or talk about.

> A _rolling stone_ [complete subject] gathers no moss.

> A rolling _stone_ [simple subject] gathers no moss.

■ The term *predicate* can apply either to the key word in the predicate *(simple predicate)* or to that key word along with all the other words that relate to it *(complete predicate)*. The key word in the predicate is always a VERB and, in fact, is usually referred to as, simply, the "verb." It does one of two things: It expresses an action performed by the subject, or it joins with another word in the predicate to indicate the condition or state of being of the subject.

> The early bird _gets the worm_ [complete predicate].

> The early bird _gets_ [verb] the worm. (expresses an action)

> Silence _is golden_ [complete predicate].

> Silence _is_ [verb] golden. (Joins with another word in the predicate to describe the condition of the subject.)

■ Every subject, by definition, must have at least one verb, and every verb must have at least one subject. The sentence itself, however, can contain more than one set of subjects and their verbs.

When the *going* [subject] *gets* [verb] tough, the *tough* [subject] *get* [verb] going.

3. THE COMPLEMENT: Finishing touches

Definition. The COMPLEMENT is the word or words in the predicate sometimes needed to complete a thought that has been only partially formed by the SUBJECT and its VERB.

A closer look. The complement can complete a thought in one of two ways:

■ It can receive the action of the verb, in which case it is known as the OBJECT of the verb.

> Politics makes *strange bedfellows*. (*Strange bedfellows* completes the thought partially formed by *politics* and *makes*. It is the object of *makes*.)

■ It can join with the verb to indicate the state of being of the subject.

> Life is *sweet*. (*Sweet* completes the thought partially formed by *life* and *is*. It joins with *is* to show the state of being of *life*.)

> Time flies. (No complement needed because the subject and its verb communicate a complete thought.)

4. CLAUSES & PHRASES: Group therapy

Definition. PHRASES and CLAUSES are groups of related words within a sentence. The chief difference between them is that clauses always include a SUBJECT and a PREDICATE. Phrases do not.

> While the cat is away [clause], the mice will play [clause]. (Both groups of words contain a subject and its verb: *cat* and *is*; and *mice* and *will play*.)

> With no cat around [phrase], the mice will play [clause]. (*With no cat around* is a phrase because it does not contain a subject and verb.)

> Charity begins *at home*. [phrase]

A closer look. Here are some general observations about phrases and clauses:

■ **Dependent and independent clauses.** There are two types of clauses—DEPENDENT and INDEPENDENT. A dependent clause (sometimes referred to as a subordinate clause) cannot stand on its own: It needs another clause in the same sentence to complete the thought. An independent clause is any group of words within a sentence that could stand on its own as a complete thought.

> If it looks like a duck and quacks like a duck [dependent clause], it is a duck [independent clause].

> If winter comes [dependent clause], can spring be far behind [independent clause].

> While Nero fiddled [dependent clause], Rome burned [independent clause].

■ **Restrictive and nonrestrictive clauses.** A RESTRICTIVE clause is a dependent clause whose presence in the sentence is essential to the basic meaning of the main clause. A NONRESTRICTIVE clause is a dependent clause whose presence contributes information that may be important but is not absolutely essential to the fundamental meaning of the sentence.

We hope to complete this job *when the weather turns warmer*.(A restrictive clause: Without it, the basic meaning of the main clause would be lost.)

We hope to complete the job in July, *when the weather turns warmer*. (A nonrestrictive clause: Without it, the basic meaning of the main clause would still be intact. The clause simply adds additional information about July.)

Why it matters. The distinction between restrictive and nonrestrictive clauses is important for two reasons. First, the choice between the relative pronoun *that* or *which* depends on the type of clause it introduces: *that* for restrictive and *which* for nonrestrictive; second, commas are generally used to separate nonrestrictive clauses and phrases from the rest of the sentence but are never used for restrictive phrases and clauses.

This is the house *that Jack built*. (The clause is restrictive: It limits the meaning of *house* to one category only—the one that *Jack built*.)

This house, *which Jack built himself*, is for sale. (*Which Jack built himself* is nonrestrictive. Even without it, readers would still know which house was being referred to.)

Let he *who is without sin* cast the first stone. (*Who is without sin* is a restrictive clause. It restricts the meaning of *he* to only those who are without sin. It does not require commas.)

Frank, *who has never sinned in his life,* threw a stone this morning. (*Who has never sinned in his life* is nonrestrictive. It contributes information about Frank, but that information is not needed to identify Frank. It needs commas to set it apart from the rest of the sentence.)

Memory key. A good way to tell whether a clause is restrictive or nonrestrictive is to see what happens to the essential meaning of the main clause when the words are removed. If the meaning is lost, the clause or phrase is restrictive. If the meaning stays reasonably intact, the clause or phrase is nonrestrictive.

5. THE PARTS OF SPEECH: Class action

Definition: The PARTS OF SPEECH are the various categories into which individual words are frequently grouped, based roughly on what function the word is serving in a sentence.

A closer look. The rationale behind classifying words into these categories is that it vastly simplifies the task of setting up and following standard principles of usage. It establishes a handful of uniform standards for tens of thousands of words (based on what part of speech they represent) as opposed to having to deal with those tens of thousands of words on an individual basis, each with its own usage quirks. Some general observations:

■ There are seven principal parts of speech in English— ADJECTIVES, ADVERBS, CONJUNCTIONS, NOUNS, PREPOSITIONS, PRONOUNS, and VERBS.

■ Most words in English can operate as more than one part of speech, depending upon their intended meaning and the role they play in a sentence.

■ The meaning of a word can change depending upon which part of speech it represents.

6. THE DIFFERENCE BETWEEN ACTION AND LINKING VERBS: Matters of state

Definition. The verb in a sentence can be one of two types: action or linking. Each type can be accompanied by a helping verb.

A closer look. Action verbs express action. Linking verbs are usually built around the verb *to be* and link the subject of the sentence to another word in the predicate that describes the state of being or condition of the subject.

> We *danced* [action] the tango until midnight.

> It *is* [linking] romantic when you dance the tango ʼt midnight.

Why it matters. The type of verb in a clause or sentence (linking or action) determines whether the modifier should be an adjective or an adverb, and also has a bearing on the CASE of the pronoun.

Some observations about linking verbs:

■ The most commonly used linking verbs are forms of the verb *to be*—*is, was, am, are, could have been*, etc. But there are a handful of verbs that can operate as either action *or* linking verbs, depending upon how you use them. These include *appear, look, feel, remain, sound*, and *taste*.

An easy way to tell whether a verb that can go both ways is a linking verb or an action verb is to see what happens when you replace the verb with *seems* or with a form of the verb *to be*. If the sentence still makes sense, the verb is probably a linking verb.

> They _appeared_ suddenly. (Action: You can't substitute _were_ or _seemed_ for _appeared_.)

> The job _appears_ complete. (Linking: _Is_ or _seems_ can easily be substituted for _appears_.)

> We have _looked_ everywhere. (Action: You can't substitute _seemed_ for _looked_.)

> The situation _looks_ good. (Linking: _Is_ or _seems_ can easily be substituted for _looks_.)

■ Modifiers that follow linking verbs are ADJECTIVES. Modifiers that precede or follow action verbs are AD-VERBS.

> We have always _worked successfully_ with small groups. (action verb and adverb)

> Our work with small groups _has_ always _been successful_. (linking verb and adjective)

■ A pronoun that follows a linking verb is in the SUB-JECTIVE CASE. A pronoun that follows an action verb is in the OBJECTIVE CASE.

> It _was she_ who asked to be in the tango contest. (linking verb followed by a pronoun in the subjective case)

> Please _tell her_ I want to _see her_. (action verbs followed by pronouns that are in the objective case)

7. THE DIFFERENCE BETWEEN VERBS AND VERBALS: Changing stripes

Definition. A VERBAL is a word or phrase that is built around a verb but that functions as either a NOUN or a MODIFIER. The three main verbals in English are the INFINITIVE, the GERUND, and the PARTICIPLE.

A closer look. Here's a brief description of each verbal.

GERUND. A noun formed by adding *-ing* to the root form of a verb.

> *Flying* to Bratislava is not my idea of a terrific time. (*Flying* is a gerund built from the verb *fly*. It operates in this sentence as the subject of the true verb *is*.)

> *Living* well is the best revenge. (*Living* is a gerund built from the verb *live*. It operates as the subject of the verb *is*.)

INFINITIVE. A verb preceded by *to*. It often operates as a noun.

> *To err* is human. *To forgive* is divine. (*To err* and *to forgive* are infinitives. The true verb in each sentence is *is*.)

PARTICIPLE. An adjective (and occasionally a noun) formed by adding *-ed* or *-ing* to a verb.

> Inga is a *changed* person since she came back from Bratislava. (*Changed* is a *participle* based on the verb *change*. It is used here to modify *person*.)

> We live in *changing* times. (*Changing* is a *participle* based on the verb *change* but is used here to modify *times*.)

Why it matters. The most important thing to keep in mind about verbals is not to confuse them with true verbs ending in either *-ing* or *-ed*. A true verb will always have a subject and will either express an action or join with another verb to describe the condition of the subject. A verbal, on the other hand, can *be* a subject or can modify a subject but it can never take the place of a true verb. Notice the differences in the following examples:

> People *were dancing* last night until 2 a.m. (*Dancing* here is a true verb, along with the helping verb *were*. It expresses an action. Its subject is *people.*)

> The *dancing* on the upstairs floor kept me up all night. (*Dancing* is a gerund. It operates as a noun and as the subject of the true verb *kept.*)

> The *dancing* contest starts at nine. (*Dancing* is a participle. It operates as an adjective modifying *contest.*)

8. THE DIFFERENCE BETWEEN ADJECTIVES AND ADVERBS: Modified goals

Definition. Adjectives and adverbs are both modifiers: words that limit the meaning or modify other words. The difference lies in the kinds of words each of them modifies.

A closer look: Some general observations about adjectives and adverbs.

■ Adjectives modify nouns or join with a linking verb to describe the condition of a subject. Adverbs modify verbs or other adverbs.

Walk *softly* [adverb] but carry a *big* [adjective] stick. (*Softly* modifies *walk*, a verb; *big* modifies *stick*, a noun.)

The market for guacamole ice cream is *soft* [adjective]. (*Soft* follows a linking verb, *is*, and describes the condition of the market.)

■ Most modifiers can function as either adverbs or adjectives. Adverbs usually end in *-ly*, but there are a handful of common adverbs that don't and several adjectives that do.

They arrived *late* [adverb]. (*Late* modifies the action verb *arrived*.)

We took a *leisurely* [adjective] stroll. (*Leisurely* modifies the noun *stroll*.)

■ When you want to modify an adjective, use an adverb.

That was an *unbelievably* exciting tango contest. (The adverb is needed here to modify the adjective *exciting*.)

The Parts of Speech at a Glance

Part	Main Job	Example	Key Usage Points
Adjectives	Add meaning to or modify nouns and pronouns.	The *maintenance* staff has given the *new* machine a *thorough* inspection.	■ Undergo slight changes in form when used in comparisons. (Example: *fast, faster, fastest*) ■ Usually *precede* the nouns they modify.
Adverbs	Add to or modify the meaning of verbs, adjectives, or other adverbs.	*Yesterday* the staff *thoroughly* inspected the new machine.	■ Usually end in *-ly,* but with many common exceptions. ■ Can either precede or follow the verbs they modify.
Articles	Help define nouns.	*The* maintenance staff has given *the* new machine *a* thorough inspection.	■ *An* precedes words that begin with a vowel (*a, e, i, o, u*) sound. ■ A precedes words that begin with a consonant (all other letters) sound.

The Parts of Speech at a Glance (con't.)

Part	Main Job	Example	Key Usage Points
Conjunctions	Connect words, phrases, and clauses.	The maintenance staff *and* the government team have inspected the new machine, *but* the company still wants to wait until next week to start it.	■ Some conjunctions (*however*, *but*, *moreover*, etc.) not only connect phrases and clauses, but also signal the relationship between the ideas.
Interjections	Show surprise or emotion.	*No!* We do not want anything done until next week.	■ Should be used sparingly in business.
Nouns	Name persons, places, things, and ideas.	As a *result* of the *company's* new *policy*, the *machine* needs a daily *inspection*.	■ Require slight changes to distinguish singular from plural and to indicate when the noun is possessive. ■ Must begin with a capital letter when referring to specific persons, places, and things.

(con't.)

The Parts of Speech at a Glance (con't.)

Part	Main Job	Example	Key Usage Points
Prepositions	Establish a relationship between a noun and the rest of the sentence.	*According to* company policy, the new machine should be inspected *during* working hours.	■ Form never changes regardless of the role they play in the sentence. ■ Usually combine with nouns or noun equivalents and modifiers to form prepositional phrases.
Pronouns	Substitute for nouns.	*This* is the first time *we* have conducted a full-scale inspection of the machine.	■ Frequently change their forms according to the role they play in the sentence and according to the person (*I, you, he, she, it*), number (singular or plural), and gender (masculine or feminine) of the word for which they are substituting.
Verbs	Express action or state of being.	This *is* the first time we *have conducted* a full-scale inspection of the machine.	■ Form usually changes to reflect person and time. ■ Should always agree with their subject nouns or pronouns in number.

Glossary

(Note: All terms in SMALL CAPITALS are defined elsewhere in the glossary.)

Action verb.   One of the three types of verbs (the other two are HELPING and LINKING). It describes any verb (e.g., *talk, run, drive,* etc.) that expresses an action.

Active voice.   One of the two ways that ACTION VERBS can be expressed, based on the way the word relates to its SUBJECT and OBJECT. In active voice constructions, the subject of the verb (i.e., the performer of the action) is also the subject of the sentence. *See also* PASSIVE VOICE.

Adjective.   One of the PARTS OF SPEECH. Its principal job is to describe or limit the meaning of a NOUN or PRONOUN. Adjectives generally answer one of three questions: Which one? What kind? How many? *See also* ADVERB.

Adverb.   One of the PARTS OF SPEECH. Its principal function is to limit or broaden the meaning of a VERB or ADJECTIVE. Adverbs generally answer one of three questions: How? When? Where?

Agreement.   A term used in connection with SUBJECTS and their VERBS, and with PRONOUNS and their ANTECEDENTS. Subjects and their verbs agree when they both represent the same NUMBER. Pronouns and their antecedents agree when the pronoun is expressed in the same NUMBER, PERSON, and GENDER as the antecedent.

Antecedent. The word (usually a NOUN or PRONOUN) for which a pronoun is being substituted. In the sentence, "Inga did her best," the antecedent of *her* is *Inga*. A basic principle of pronoun usage is that pronouns must agree with their antecedents in PERSON, NUMBER, and GENDER.

Apostrophe. A punctuation mark (') that has two main jobs: to indicate possession in a NOUN (*Lucy's* friend) or to substitute for the missing letters in a CONTRACTION (We *can't* go next week).

Appositive. A word or PHRASE that follows a NOUN or PRONOUN and acts, in effect, as a mirror image of that word. Example: Inga, *my good friend*, will be visiting us next week.

Case. The specific role a word—usually a PRONOUN—is playing in a sentence: whether it is the subject of a verb (SUBJECTIVE CASE), the object of a verb or preposition (OBJECTIVE CASE), or the possessive modifier (POSSESSIVE CASE). Personal pronouns change their forms to correspond to the case of the pronoun.

Clause. A group of related words that includes a VERB and its SUBJECT. There are two types: DEPENDENT and INDEPENDENT.

Collective noun. A NOUN whose singular form refers to a group of persons, places, things, or actions. Examples: *team, staff, committee, jury*. Collective nouns usually require the SINGULAR form of a VERB.

Colon. A punctuation mark (:) whose main job is to create a pause that alerts the reader to look ahead.

Comma. A punctuation mark (,) whose main job is to indicate natural pauses between WORDS, CLAUSES, and PHRASES.

Common noun. One of two major classes of NOUNS. The

term refers to nonspecific persons, places, things, or activities. It begins with a lowercase letter. *See also* PROPER NOUN.

Complement.   The word or group of words in a sentence that completes a thought that has been partially formed by the SUBJECT and its VERB. Complements do one of two things: They receive the action of the verb, or they follow a linking verb and refer back to the subject.

Complex sentence.   A sentence that includes at least one DEPENDENT CLAUSE, in addition to an INDEPENDENT CLAUSE.

Compound sentence.   A sentence that consists of at least two INDEPENDENT CLAUSES usually connected by a CONJUNCTION. The independent clauses in a compound sentence are generally separated by a COMMA, a SEMICOLON, or, in some cases, a COLON.

Compound subject.   A term used to describe the subject of any sentence in which the SUBJECT consists of two or more words.

Conjunction.   One of the PARTS OF SPEECH. Its main job is to connect words and groups of words within a SENTENCE.

Contraction.   A word formed by combining two words and shortening the combination by replacing one or more of the letters with an APOSTROPHE.

Dash.   A punctuation mark (—) that produces a sharp break between elements in a SENTENCE.

Dependent clause.   A group of related words that includes a SUBJECT and PREDICATE but cannot stand alone as a complete thought. Also known as a subordinate clause.

Exclamation point.   A punctuation mark (!) used to give added emphasis to a statement.

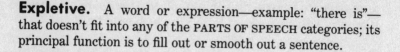

Expletive. A word or expression—example: "there is"—that doesn't fit into any of the PARTS OF SPEECH categories; its principal function is to fill out or smooth out a sentence.

Future perfect tense. One of the six TENSES of VERBS. It expresses an action or helps to express a state of being that will be completed in the future but before some other event, as in "By the time I get to Bratislava, Dimitri *will* already *have gone.*"

Future tense. One of the six TENSES of VERBS. It covers actions that will be taking place at some time in the future, as in "We *will introduce* the new ice cream flavor next week."

Gender. A term used in connection with PRONOUNS to distinguish words that relate to men (masculine) or women (feminine).

Gerund. One of the three main types of VERBALS. It operates as a NOUN and is formed by adding the SUFFIX *-ing* to a verb.

Helping verb. A category of VERBS whose main job is to join with other verbs to express an action or state of being. Common helping verbs include *is, are, were,* and *have.*

Hyphen. A punctuation mark (-) whose principal job is to join two words together to form a new word.

Imperative. One of the three MOODS of VERBS. A verb is in the imperative mood when it expresses a command.

Indefinite pronoun. A PRONOUN that has a nonspecific ANTECEDENT. Examples: *one, some, anyone,* and *somebody.*

Independent clause. A group of related words within a SENTENCE that has a SUBJECT and PREDICATE and can stand on its own as a complete thought.

Indicative mood. The most commonly used of the three MOODS of verbs. A verb is in the indicative mood when it helps express a general statement or a question.

Indirect quotation. A quotation that has been paraphrased rather than presented word for word. It does not require QUOTATION MARKS.

Infinitive. A VERBAL formed by preceding the root form of the VERB with *to*.

Irregular verb. Any verb whose PRINCIPAL PARTS undergo changes that follow no set pattern. *See also* REGULAR VERB.

Linking verb. A verb—usually a form of *to be*—that connects the SUBJECT to a word that describes the condition or state of being of the subject.

Modifier. A word that describes or brings into a more limited perspective another word. The two common categories of modifiers are ADVERBS and ADJECTIVES.

Mood. A term used to distinguish the various types of attitudes behind a statement. In certain situations, as in the SUBJUNCTIVE mood, it can affect the ending of a verb.

Nonrestrictive clause. A RELATIVE CLAUSE that contributes information in a SENTENCE but is not absolutely essential to the fundamental meaning of the sentence. Nonrestrictive clauses are usually introduced by *which* (or *who*, if the ANTECEDENT is a person) and are set off from the rest of the SENTENCE by COMMAS.

Notional agreement. A principle of SUBJECT and VERB AGREEMENT that applies, in particular, to NOUNS and PRONOUNS that can be thought of as singular or plural, depending on the number the speaker or writer is referring to.

Noun. A part of speech whose main job is to express the names of persons, places, things, or ideas. *See also* COMMON NOUN, PROPER NOUN.

Number. A term used in connection with NOUNS, PRONOUNS, and VERBS to indicate whether a word represents one thing (SINGULAR) or more than one (PLURAL).

Object. The term applied to any word in a sentence that receives the action of a VERB or comes at the end of a PREPOSITIONAL PHRASE.

Object of a preposition. A NOUN or PRONOUN that follows a PREPOSITION, forming a PREPOSITIONAL PHRASE. Examples: in the *morning;* around the *corner;* over the *hill.*

Object of a verb. A NOUN, PRONOUN, or PHRASE that receives the action of a verb. Example: Haste makes *waste.*

Objective case. A term used to classify a PRONOUN that is the OBJECT of either a VERB or a PREPOSITION.

Parentheses. Punctuation marks ( ) used to set off groups of words that represent a break in thought from the rest of the SENTENCE.

Parenthetical clause or phrase. A group of words within a SENTENCE that contributes information that is related to the main idea of the sentence but can be removed without changing the basic meaning of a sentence. Parenthetical CLAUSES and PHRASES either are enclosed within parentheses or dashes or are separated from the rest of the sentence by COMMAS.

Participial phrase. A group of related words that contains a PARTICIPLE.

Participle. One of three kinds of VERBALS. It is formed by adding *-ing* or *-ed* to the root form of the VERB, and it operates primarily as an ADJECTIVE.

Parts of speech. The various categories into which words are grouped, based roughly on what function they play in a sentence. *See* ADJECTIVE, ADVERB, CONJUNCTION, NOUN, PREPOSITION, PRONOUN, and VERB.

Passive voice. A way of expressing an ACTION VERB so that the SUBJECT of the VERB is the receiver and not the doer of the action, as in "The plan *was adopted* by the committee last week."

Past participle. One of the PRINCIPAL PARTS of verbs. It is the form used in all the PERFECT TENSES.

Past perfect tense. One of the six TENSES of VERBS. It is used to express action or a state of being completed in the past before some other past action or event.

Past tense. One of the six TENSES of VERBS. It covers an action or state of being completed at a definite time in the past.

Perfect tenses. Three of the six VERB TENSES (PRESENT PERFECT, PAST PERFECT, FUTURE PERFECT). All use some form of the verb *have* as a helping verb.

Period. A punctuation mark (.) whose main job is to indicate the end of a SENTENCE that expresses a statement or a command.

Person. A term used in connection with VERBS and PRONOUNS. It indicates whether the SUBJECT or OBJECT of the VERB is the speaker *(first person)*, the person being spoken to *(second person)*, or the person, place, or thing being spoken about *(third person)*.

Personal pronoun. A category of PRONOUNS that refers to people. Examples: *I, you, he, she, we, they.*

Phrase. A group of closely related words that modifies a NOUN or VERB but does not contain a SUBJECT and a PREDICATE. There are several categories of phrases, including PREPOSITIONAL PHRASES, GERUNDS, and INFINITIVES.

Plural. A term used with NOUNS, PRONOUNS, and VERBS to indicate that more than one person, place, or thing is being referred to.

Possessive case. A term used occasionally with NOUNS, but more often with PRONOUNS, to indicate ownership. The punctuation mark used to indicate possession (except with pronouns) is the APOSTROPHE.

Predicate. One of the two major components of a SENTENCE. It includes all the words—and, in particular, the verb—that relate to the subject's state of being or any action taken by the subject.

Predicate adjective. An adjective complement that follows a LINKING VERB and completes the meaning of the CLAUSE or SENTENCE by describing the SUBJECT. Example: The dinner was *cold.*

Prefix. A group of letters that is added to the beginning of a word to create a new word or to alter the word's meaning.

Preposition. A part of speech whose main job is to show the relationship between a NOUN and some other word in the sentence.

Prepositional phrase. A PHRASE consisting of a PREPOSITION and its OBJECT (usually a NOUN or PRONOUN). Its main job is to modify, and it can function as either an ADJECTIVE or an ADVERB.

Present perfect tense. One of the six TENSES of VERBS. It covers actions or states of being that have only recently been completed or that are still going on, as in "We *have been working* steadily for the past two weeks."

Present tense.   One of the six TENSES of VERBS. It covers an action or state of being that is currently going on. It is also used for statements that express general ideas or universal truths.

Principal parts of verbs.   The basic VERB forms on which all other verb forms are based. These forms are the PRESENT TENSE, the PAST TENSE, and the PAST PARTICIPLE.

Pronoun.   A part of speech whose function is to substitute for nouns. Common pronouns include *I, me, you, he, him, she, her, they, them.*

Proper noun.   One of two major classes of NOUNS. It includes nouns that name specific persons, places, or things, and it always begins with a capital letter. *See also* COMMON NOUN.

Question mark.   The punctuation mark (?) used to indicate that a sentence is asking a question.

Quotation marks.   Punctuation marks ("/") used primarily to set off statements that are attributed to someone other than the person writing and are repeated word for word.

Reflexive verb.   A VERB whose SUBJECT and OBJECT refer to the same person or thing. It is almost always followed by a PRONOUN that ends in the suffix *-self.*

Regular verb.   A category of VERBS so-called because they form their PRINCIPAL PARTS in the same way: by adding *-ed* to form both the past and past participle forms.

Relative clause.   A DEPENDENT CLAUSE introduced by any of the three relative PRONOUNS—*that, which,* or *who.*

Restrictive clause. A RELATIVE CLAUSE that so limits the meaning of the sentence that without the clause the essential meaning of the sentence would be lost. Restrictive clauses are usually introduced by *that* or *who*. *See also* NONRESTRICTIVE CLAUSE.

Semicolon. A punctuation mark (;) that can be used instead of a COMMA to separate INDEPENDENT CLAUSES in a COMPOUND SENTENCE.

Sentence. A group of words that can stand on its own as a completed thought. It almost always contains a SUBJECT and PREDICATE. It begins with a capital letter and ends with a PERIOD, a QUESTION MARK, or an EXCLAMATION POINT.

Singular. The term used to distinguish a NOUN, PRONOUN, or VERB that refers to one person, place, or thing from a noun, pronoun, or verb that refers to more than one. *See also* PLURAL.

Subject. The word or group of words in a SENTENCE that represents what person, place, thing, or idea the sentence is about.

Subjective case. One of the three CASES of pronouns. Sometimes referred to as the nominative case, it refers mainly to pronouns that operate as the subjects of verbs or that follow linking verbs.

Subjunctive. One of the three moods of VERBS. Verbs are in this mood when a statement expresses a wish, a doubt, a fear, or something contrary to fact.

Suffix. A group of letters that can be added to the end of a word to form either a new word or a variation of the root word.

Synonym. A word close enough in meaning to another word that it can be used in its place.

Tense.   A term used with VERBS that denotes the time frame of an action. There are six tenses in English: PRESENT, PAST, FUTURE, PRESENT PERFECT, PAST PERFECT, and FUTURE PERFECT.

Verb.   One of the PARTS OF SPEECH. Its function is to express an action or join with another word to show the state of being of the subject.

Verbal.   A word or PHRASE that is built around a VERB but functions as a PART OF SPEECH other than a verb. The three verbals in English are INFINITIVES, GERUNDS, and PARTICIPLES.

Bibliography

Bernstein, Theodore M. *The Careful Writer.* New York: Atheneum, 1979.

Claiborne, Robert. *Saying What You Mean.* New York: Ballantine, 1986.

Craig, Ruth P., and Vincent F. Hopper. *1001 Pitfalls in English Grammar.* Woodbury, NY: Barron's Educational Series, 1986.

Curme, George O. *A Grammar of the English Language,* 6th ed. Essex, CT: Verbatim, 1986.

Fitchen, Allen, sr. ed. *The Chicago Manual of Style,* 13th ed. Chicago: University of Chicago Press, 1982.

Follett, Wilson. *Modern American Usage.* New York: Hill & Wang, 1966.

Fowler, H. W. *A Dictionary of Modern English Usage.* London: Oxford University Press, 1983.

Freeman, Morton S. *The Wordwatcher's Guide to Good Writing & Grammar.* Cincinnati, OH: Writer's Digest, 1990.

Graves, Robert, and Alan Hodge. *The Use and Abuse of the English Language.* New York: Paragon, 1990.

Johnson, Edward D. *The Handbook of Good English.* New York: Pocket Books, 1991.

Lewis, Norman. *30 Days to Better English.* New York: New American Library, 1985.

Morris, William, ed. *The American Heritage Dictionary of the English Language.* Boston, MA: Houghton Mifflin, 1981.

Sabin, William A. *The Gregg Reference Manual*, 6th ed. New York: McGraw-Hill, 1985.

Safire, William. *I Stand Corrected*. New York: Times Books, 1984.

Strunk, William, Jr., and E. B. White. *The Elements of Style*, 3rd ed. New York: Macmillan, 1979.

Webster's Dictionary of English Usage, Springfield, MA: Merriam-Webster, Inc., 1989.

Webster's Ninth New Collegiate Dictionary, Springfield, MA: Merriam-Webster, Inc., 1991.

Index

For a free copy of the newsletter *Saying It Better,* or for information about Grammar for Smart People courses, seminars, corporate programs and on-line options, write Communications Dynamics International Inc., P.O. Box 5156, Westport, CT 06881, or call (203) 454-5889.

51 Edgeworth Avenue
Portland, ME 04103
207-310-8774